And What Rough Beast

Poems at the End of the Century

Edited by Robert McGovern and Stephen Haven

The Ashland Poetry Press
Ashland University
Ashland, Ohio 44805

Copyright © 1999 by the Ashland Poetry Press

All rights reserved. Except for brief quotations in critical reviews, this book, or parts thereof, must not be reproduced in any form without permission in writing from the publisher. For further information, contact the Ashland Poetry Press, Ashland University, Ashland, OH 44805.

Printed in the United States of America

ISBN 0-912592-41-9

Library of Congress Card Number 98-74622

Cover: "Surely Some Revelation is at Hand" (W.B. Yeats, 1920), by John Thrasher.

 The Ohio Arts Council helped fund this organization with state tax dollars to encourage economic growth, educational excellence and cultural enrichment for all Ohioans.

Acknowledgments

Addonizio, Kim. "Target," originally appeared in *Alaska Quarterly Review*; Atkins, Russell. "Heroic Vigil," originally appeared in *Poetry Now*; Baker, David. "Mid-west: Ode," originally appeared in *The Georgia Review*; Barnes, Jim. "Pyramid," originally appeared in *Paris* (University of Illinois Press, 1997); Battin, Wendy. "The News From Mars," originally appeared in *Little Apocalypse* (Ashland Poetry Press, 1997); Bell, Marvin. "Sounds of the Resurrected Dead Man's Footsteps #6," and "Sounds of the Resurrected Dead Man's Footsteps # 3," originally appeared in *Prairie Schooner*; "Sounds of the Resurrected Dead Man's Footsteps #13," originally appeared in *Green Mountains Review*; Bellamy, Joe David. "Light Years," originally appeared in *Tar River Poetry*; Bogen, Don. "Among Appliances," originally appeared in *The Known World* (Wesleyan/New England, 1997); Booth, Philip. "Late Wakings," originally appeared in *The Georgia Review*; Bruce, Debra. "Follow-Up Exam," originally appeared in *What Wind Will Do* (Miami University Press of Ohio, 1997); Buckley, Christopher. "Opera," originally appeared in *Fall From Grace* (BkMk Press of the University of Missouri Kansas City, 1998); Budy, Andrea Hollander. "The Hunters," originally appeared in *DoubleTake*; Castro, Michael. "Chili Mac," originally appeared in *Pittsburgh Quarterly*; Chaberek, Ed. 'The American," appeared simultaneously in *Crimson Lear* & *Superior Poetry News*; Chichetto, James Wm. "Blind Veteran (Korean War)," originally appeared in *The Colorado Review*; Clinton, DeWitt. "Touring the Holocaust," originally appeared in *The Southern California Anthology (1995)*; Cording, Robert. "Dust," originally appeared in *Sewanee Review*; Dacey, Philip. "Disney: The Wall," originally appeared in *Mid-American Review*; "On a Contributor's Note for William Stafford," originally appeared in *Crab Orchard Review*; Davis, Melody. "It Only Starts," originally appeared in *Poetry*; Domina, Lynn. "In Lonely Exile Here," originally appeared in *Many Mountains Moving*; Ehrhart, W.D. "Guns," originally appeared in *The Distance We Travel* (Adastra Press, 1993); Elledge, Jim. "606 E. Front St., Bloomington, IL 61701," originally appeared in *Zone 3*; Emmons, Jeanne. "Oil Slick," originally appeared in *Rootbound* (New Rivers Press, 1998); Espada, Martin. "Thanksgiving," originally appeared in *Ploughshares*; Fishman, Charles. "Natural Selection," originally appeared in *College English*; Fleming, Deborah. "Strip Mines," originally appeared in *Organization and Environment*; Fried, Philip. "Catechism," originally appeared in *Quantum Genesis and Other Poems* (Zohar Press, 1997); Frost, Richard. "What I Did In the War," originally appeared in *Cimarron Review*; Fulton, Alice. "About Face," and "A Little Heart To Heart With The Horizon," originally appeared in *Sensual Math* (W.W. Norton, 1995); Gallaher, Cynthia. "Gulf Sheep," originally appeared in *Thorntree Press Anthology*; Gonzalez-T., Cesar A. "Tocayo," originally appeared in *San Diego Writers Monthly*; Graham, Matthew. "Cold War," originally appeared in *River Styx*; Grennan, Eamon. "Colour Shot," originally appeared in *As If It Matters* (Graywolf, 1992); Hawkins, Hunt. "G-Man," originally appeared in *Southern Review*; "The Invisible Hand Meets the Dead Hand," originally appeared in *The Minnesota Review*; Heller, Michael. "To Postmodernity," originally appeared in *Wordflow* (Talisman House, 1997); Hershon, Robert. "Light and Dark, East and West," originally appeared in *Verse*; Hilbert, Donna. "Vanguard Barbie Gets Fitted," originally appeared in *Panic*; Hirshfield, Jane. "Jasmine," originally appeared in *The Lives of the Heart* (HarperCollins, 1997); Hoffman, Daniel. "In The Gallery," originally appeared in *The New Yorker*; Iodice, Ruth G. "Towards Ithaca," originally appeared in *Blue Unicorn*; Jaffe, Maggie. "For Lewis B. Puller, Jr.," originally appeared in *7th Circle* (Cedar Hill Publications, 1998); Jauss, David. "Homage To John Cage," originally appeared in *Improvising Rivers* (Cleveland State University Press, 1995); Kennedy, X.J. "Then and Now," originally appeared in *Blue Unicorn*; "For Allen Ginsberg," originally appeared in *Poetry*; Kronen, Steve. "For L, Born August 6, 1945," originally appeared in *The Threepenny Review*; Krysl, Marilyn. "Suite for Kokodicholai, Sri Lanka," originally appeared in *Warscape With Lovers* (Cleveland State University Press, 1997); Timothy Liu. "Billions Served" and "The Presence of an Absence in a Midwest Town" are reprinted from *Say Goodnight*. Reprinted by permission of Copper Canyon Press, PO Box 271, Port Townsend, WA 98368; Locke, Edward. "Directing the Future," originally appeared in *Verve*; Loden, Rachel. "Checkers Rising," originally appeared in *New American Writing*; "My Night With Philip Larkin," originally appeared in *B City*; Logghe, Joan. "War Crimes," originally appeared in *What Makes A Woman Beautiful?* (Pennywhistle, 1993); Loo, Jeffrey. "For Etheridge Knight (1931–March 10, 1991)," originally appeared in *African American Review*; Martin, Charles. "Stanzas after Endgame," originally appeared in *What the Darkness Proposes*; McAlpine, Katherine. "Yellow Submarine Homesick Blues Revisited," originally appeared in *Amelia*; McClanahan, Rebecca. "Writers' Conference, Last Dance," originally appeared in *Laurel Review*; McDonald, Walt. "Once You've Been to War," originally appeared in *The Flying Dutchman* (Ohio State University Press, 1987); "The War in Bosnia," originally appeared in *Meridian*; Meinke, Peter. "Greenhouse Statistics," originally appeared in *Scars* (University of Pittsburgh Press, 1996); reprinted by permission of University of Pittsburgh Press; Mott, Michael. "In Memory of William Stafford 1914-1993," originally appeared in *Sewanee Review*; Muske, Carol. "To the Muse," & "Field Trip," are reprinted by permission of Penguin Books from *An Octive Above Thunder: New and Selecaated Poems* (Penguin Books, 1997); Nims, John Frederick. "Moses Descending," originally appeared in *Chronicles*; Nurske, D. "Payless," originally appeared in *Grand Street*; O'Halloran, Jamie. "No Angel," originally appeared in *Blue Satellite*; Overton, Ron. "Two Stories," originally appeared in *Hanging Loose*; Pastan, Linda. "The News of the World," originally appeared in *Carnival Evening: New and Selected Poems 1968-1998* (W.W. Norton, 1998); "Near the End of the Century," originally appeared in *The GW Review*; Peacock, Molly. "Goodbye Hello in the East Village," originally appeared in *Original Love* (W.W. Norton 1995); Pennant, Edmund. "Mahane Yehuda," originally appeared in *Jewish Frontier*; Piirto, Jane. "Fraternity Bar in Athens, Georgia," originally appeared in *Between the Memory and the Experience* (Sisu Press, 1996); Ray, David. "An Incident in Union, Carolina," originally appeared in *New Letters*; Ray, Judy. "Scheherazade," originally appeared in *The Chariton Review*; Reiss, James. "Skimming Toward Blue," originally appeared in *Ten Thousand Mornings*; Rogers, Pattiann. "The Kingdom of Heaven," originally appeared in *Eating Bread and Honey* (Milkweed Editions, 1997) and is reprinted with permission of the author; Root, William Pitt. "Writing Late Through the Night of the Tiananmen Square Massacre," originally appeared in *Many Mountains Moving*; Schulman, Grace. "Prayer" originally appeared in *Poetry*; "The Wedding," originally appeared in *For That Day Only* (Sheep Meadow Press, 1994); Schwartz, Ruth. "The City," originally appeared in *Americas Review*; Sherman, John. "Cages," originally appeared in *Reading Around Indianapolis*; Shomer, Enid. "Writing A Formal Poem the Winter After Your Death," originally appeared in *Black Drum* (University of Arkansas Press); Skinner, Jeffrey. "Late Afternoon, Late in the Twentieth Century," originally appeared in *Ohio Review*; Spires, Elizabeth. "1999," originally appeared in *American Poetry Review*; Suk, Julie. "Leaving the World We've Loved Speechless," originally appeared in *Poetry*; Terris, Susan. "Boxcar at the Holocaust Museum," originally appeared in *Noe Valley Voice*; Tham, Hilary. "A True Story," originally appeared in *Men & Other Strange Myths* (Three Continents Press, 1994); Thompson, Phyllis Hoge. "Beauty," originally appeared in *ORL Anniversary Anthology 1995*; Trowbridge, William. "His Greatest Moments," originally appeared in *Great River Review*; Uyematsu, Amy. "The Ten Million Flames of Los Angeles," originally appeared in *Flash-Bopp*; Waters, Michael. "Miles Weeping," originally appeared in *American Poetry Review*; Weiner, Joshua. "Tokens," originally appeared in *The Nation*; Welch, Don. "The Unicorn," originally appeared in *Epoch*; Wheeler, Jackson. "Sleeping With the Third World," originally appeared in *Swimming Past Iceland*; Wright, Carolyne. "The Peace Corps Volunteer Comes Home," originally appeared in *From A White Woman's Journal* (Water Mark Press Chapbook, 1985).

Contents

Kim Addonizio:
    Target/1
Russell Atkins:
    Heroic Vigil/2
David Baker:
    Midwest: Ode/3
J.T. Barbarese:
    Diorama/4
Jim Barnes:
    The Glass Pyramid/4
Marilyn Bates:
    Frozen Sperm & Frozen Eggs/6
Wendy Battin:
    The News from Mars/7
Grace Bauer:
    Flowers in February/9
Marvin Bell:
    Sounds of the Resurrected Dead Man's Footsteps #3/10
    Sounds of the Resurrected Dead Man's Footsteps #6/11
    Sounds of the Resurrected Dead Man's Footsteps #13/13
Joe David Bellamy:
    Light Years/14
Don Bogen:
    Among Appliances/14
Harold Bond:
    Living with Pain/16
Philip Booth:
    Late Wakings/17
Perry Brass:
    Two San Francisco Poems/17
Debra Bruce:
    Follow-up Exam/19
Joseph Bruchac:
    Men of the Forest/20
Christopher Buckley:
    Opera/21

Andrea Hollander Budy:
    The Hunters/22
Grace Butcher:
    The Last War/23
Lucas Carpenter:
    ByeByeBlackbird/24
Hayden Carruth:
    Small Fundamental Essay/25
Turner Cassity:
    Performing *Le Prophète,* or, Meyerbeer in Texas/26
Michael Castro:
    Chili Mac/26
Ed Chaberek:
    The American/27
James Wm. Chichetto:
    Blind Veteran (Korean War)/28
Paul Christensen:
    Ode to Dolly/28
    African Elegy/30
David Citino:
    Ode to Billie Dove/31
DeWitt Clinton:
    Touring the Holocaust/32
Carole Cohen:
    Approaching the Internet/36
Phyllis K. Collier:
    Vanishing/37
Robert Cording:
    Dust/38
David Curtis:
    Feeling/39
Philip Dacey:
    Disney: The Wall/40
    On a Contributor's Note for William Stafford/41
Melody Davis:
    It Only Starts/42
R.P. Dickey:
    I Have a Daydream Tonight/43

Lynn Domina:
    In Lonely Exile Here/44
Susan Donnelly:
    Harpo/45
William Doreski:
    Manhattan Valhalla/45
Thomas Dorsett:
    Farewell, Abbie Hoffman/47
Peter Kane Dufault:
    DNA/48
W.D. Ehrhart:
    Guns/48
Susan Eisenberg:
    Tell Me/49
Jim Elledge:
    606 E. Front St., Bloomington, IL 61701/51
Jeanne Emmons:
    Oil Slick/52
Martín Espada:
    Thanksgiving/52
Rhina P. Espaillat:
    Bra/54
Pat Falk:
    On the Beach/54
Jim Fairhall:
    McNamara/55
Charles Fishman:
    Natural Selection/57
Doug Flaherty:
    Default Mode/57
Deborah Fleming:
    Strip Mines/58
Stewart Florsheim:
    Recent Findings/59
Peter Fogo:
    Eating Monkeys/60
Brett Foster:
    Armistice to Music/61

Linda Nemec Foster:
    Sitting in America at the End of the Century/62
Philip Fried:
    Catechism/64
Richard Frost:
    What I Did in the War/64
Alice Fulton:
    About Face/66
    A Little Heart to Heart with the Horizon/67
Cynthia Gallaher:
    Gulf Sheep/68
César A. González-T.:
    Tocayo/69
Darcy Gottlieb:
    This Difficult and Beautiful Life/70
Matthew Graham:
    Cold War/71
Alvin Greenberg:
    "me and my shadow"/72
William Greenway:
    Mississippi Moon/74
Eamon Grennan:
    Colour Shot/75
Gordon Grigsby:
    Shine, Perishing Empire/76
Mac Hammond:
    The Year 2000/77
Stephen Haven:
    Near the Millennium/77
    Elegy for Larry Levis/80
Hunt Hawkins:
    G-Man/80
    Invisible Hand Meets the Dead Hand/81
George Held:
    Inauguration (1997) Sestina/82
Michael Heller:
    To Postmodernity/83
Robert Hershon:
    Light and Dark, East and West/84

Donna Hilbert:
>Vanguard Barbie Gets Fitted/85

Jane Hirshfield:
>Jasmine/86

Daniel Hoffman:
>In the Gallery/86

Frances Hunter:
>March 1992/87

Kathleen Iddings:
>Maple Rocker/88

Ruth G. Iodice:
>Towards Ithaca/89

Bonnie Jacobson:
>Waving to Nemerov/89

Maggie Jaffe:
>For Lewis B. Puller, Jr./89

David Jauss:
>Homage to John Cage/90

Vincent Katz:
>Ciao, Jim/91

X.J. Kennedy:
>Then and Now/92
>For Allen Ginsberg/93

Shirley Kishyama:
>Notre Dame, 1995/93

Carolyn Kizer:
>Fin-de-Siècle Blues/95

Steve Kronen:
>For L, Born August 6, 1945/99

Marilyn Krysl:
>Suite for Kokodicholai, Sri Lanka/100

Barbara F. Lefcowitz:
>Goodbye 20th Century/102

Deena Linett:
>Peace in Ireland/103

P.H. Liotta:
>On the Failure Named Bosnia/105

Timothy Liu:
    Billions Served/107
    The Presence of an Absence in a Midwest Town/107
Edward Locke:
    Directing the Future/108
Rachel Loden:
    Checkers Rising/110
    My Night with Philip Larkin/110
Joan Logghe:
    War Crimes/111
Jeffrey Loo:
    For Etheridge Knight/ 112
Susan Luther:
    Hymn for the Children of Israel/116
Rick Lyon:
    Venice, Easter 1996: In Memory of Joseph Brodsky/117
Don Mager:
    The Unbearable Truth that Is Beauty/118
James Magner:
    Ritual of the Green/119
Mordecai Marcus:
    The Enduring Poet: Farewell to Stephen Spender/120
Charles Martin:
    Stanzas after *Endgame*/121
Katherine McAlpine:
    Yellow Submarine Homesick Blues Revisited/122
Rebecca McClanahan:
    Writers' Conference, Last Dance/124
David B. McCoy:
    From *The Oil War: 1991*/125
Walt McDonald:
    Once You've Been to War/126
    The War in Bosnia/127
Robert McGovern:
    Of Military Scandals/127
    Ella (1918-1996) Fitzgerald/128

Peter Meinke:
    Greenhouse Statistics/128
    Assisted Living/130
Gregory McNamee:
    Sarasvati in the New World/131
Jean Monahan:
    Dolly/132
Michael Mott:
    In Memory of William Stafford/133
Joan Murray:
    Taking the Count/134
Carol Muske:
    To the Muse/135
    Field Trip/136
Mildred J. Nash:
    An Invitation of Sorts/138
John Frederick Nims:
    Moses Descending/139
D. Nurkse:
    Payless/140
Francis O'Connor:
    The Venerable Tree/140
Jamie O'Halloran:
    No Angel/141
Adrian Oktenberg:
    Hyakutake/142
Ron Overton:
    Two Stories/143
Robert Parham:
    Swan Song for Deconstruction/143
Linda Pastan:
    The News of the World/144
    Near the End of the Century/145
Molly Peacock:
    Goodbye Hello in the East Village/145
Edmund Pennant:
    Mahane Yehuda/146
Stuart Peterfreund:
    Yom Hashoa: The Reading of the Names/147

Jane Piirto:
> Fraternity Bar in Athens, Georgia/148

David Ray:
> An Incident in Union, Carolina/149
> Progress Report/150
> Wrappings/151

Judy Ray:
> Scheherazade/151

James Reiss:
> Skimming Toward Blue/152

Pattiann Rogers:
> The Kingdom of Heaven/154

William Pitt Root:
> Writing Late Through the Night
> of the Tiananmen Square Massacre/155

Eugene Ruggles:
> Somalia Kneeling/158
> February Eleventh Nineteen Ninety–
> Nelson Mandela Walks Into Freedom/159

Grace Schulman:
> Prayer/160
> The Wedding/161

Ruth L. Schwartz:
> The City/162

Myra Shapiro:
> Columbus Circle/163

John Sherman:
> Cages/164

Enid Shomer:
> Writing a Formal Poem the Winter after Your Death/165

Jeffrey Skinner:
> Late Afternoon, Late in the Twentieth Century/166

Elizabeth Spires:
> 1999/168

Julie Suk:
> Leaving the World We've Loved Speechless/169

William Sylvester:
> Political Horn Book/170

Susan Terris:
> Boxcar at the Holocaust Museum/172

Nadja Tesich:
> My Eyes and His/173

Hilary Tham:
> A True Story/174

Phyllis Thompson:
> Beauty/174

William Trowbridge:
> His Greatest Moments/176

Lewis Turco:
> The Great Ice Storm of 'Ninety-Eight/176

Amy Uyematsu:
> The Ten Million Flames of Los Angeles/177

Julia Vinograd:
> Peace/178

Chocolate Waters:
> Anonymous/179

Michael Waters:
> Miles Weeping/181

Joshua Weiner:
> Tokens/182

Don Welch:
> The Unicorn/183

Jackson Wheeler:
> Sleeping with the Third World/184

Paul Willis:
> A Miracle/185

Mary Winters:
> Whoopee, It's 2000/185

Carolyne Wright:
> The Peace Corps Volunteer Comes Home/187

Preface

Some three decades ago, when the late Richard Snyder was senior editor at the Ashland Poetry Press, we published a book entitled *60 on the 60s–a Decade's History in Verse.* Since then, the press has published sequels on the 70s and 80s. We now offer still another sequel, the title of which we drew from William Butler Yeats' poem, "The Second Coming," in which Yeats asserts a fragmented society that is aiming toward its disintegration with the advent of the new millennium–the "rough beast" that "slouches towards Bethlehem to be born."

In this book, we make no prophecies, but we do mark the shocks and absurdities of the 90s and, by extension, of this century as a whole, and we try to anticipate something of the new millennium. We wrote in the preface to the *60s* that the anthology tries "to penetrate beyond historical fact to the artistic response that leads to a full human understanding" of our world. That book, as this, is a collection of song, and where there is song, however painful or desperate, there is hope for human salvation.

We are somewhat more ambitious in this book in facing up to the *fin de siècle* and the beginning of the new millennium, thereby taking on a larger sense of time. Through the perspective of the historical imagination, we call up parallels to what went on since 1900. The holocaust is still very much with us, as are other aspects of this century's many wars and political upheavals.

Also, the shape of the book has changed since our earlier efforts, where we organized the material chronologically. Our reading of the manuscripts submitted suggested that we could produce a phantasmagoric experience of the decade and century by the simple expedient of publishing the poems alphabetically by the poets' names, a solution we had employed in another anthology (*Scarecrow Poetry: the Muse in Post-Middle Age*).

This book is also much longer than the first three (we couldn't have done the 90s in 90 poems). The submissions were almost daunting; some 1,200 poets submitted around 12,000 poems.

We should like to thank those who have contributed to the making of this book, including Nancy Grimm, production coordinator, Mary Snyder, technical assistance, Robert Cummiskey, student assistant, and artist John Thrasher for providing the cover. A special thanks goes to the Ohio Arts Council for a generous grant towards the book's production.

–Robert McGovern and Stephen Haven

Kim Addonizio

Target

It feels so good to shoot a gun,
to stand with your legs apart
holding a nine millimeter in both hands
aiming at something that can't run.
Over and over I rip holes

in the paper target clamped to its hanger,
target I move closer with the flick of a switch
or so far away its center looks
like a small black planet in its white square
of space. It feels good to nestle a clip

of bullets against the heel of your hand,
to ratchet one into the chamber
and cock the hammer back and fire, the recoil
surging along your arms as the muzzle kicks up, as you keep
control. It's so good you no longer wonder

why some boys lift them from bottom drawers and boxes
at the backs of closets, and drive fast into lives
they won't finish, lean from their car windows and
let go a few rounds into whatever's out there
just to hear what comes back: burst glass,

or the high ring of struck steel,
or maybe moans. Suddenly you want
to take the thing and hurl it into
the ocean, let it drop down through
the dark and cold until it lodges so deep

nothing could retrieve it. But you know it would
float back and wash up like a bottle
carrying a message from a dead man. You stand there
emptying it into the target until it feels
light again, and innocent. And then you reload.

Russell Atkins

Heroic Vigil

Here is a street's loomed big
wavering from theft's swift
or crept's shuddered attack.
Take a stand, a firm one
here, about eleven o'clock eved
–give the lie to stories
of rape, murder, robbery, peddled crack;
fix scoff forever on dastards
who wouldn't be caught dead here!
the glut of crime–
treat that like a snack!

Carry money, of course,
(a hundred'll do in a fat wallet)
and staunch'd against daunt
have out a Marlboro
flick it alive aplomb'd of lit;
recall explorers brave with dare,
chuckle to yourself for being alone
leisuring against abandoned hulks
broken bulldozers, cars' cadavers,
deserted school buildings

a columnist will rave of you,
citizens' groups will urge you into politics,
the mayor sign your certificate
on Public Square
                    you may
–though absent–
              make headlines

David Baker

Midwest: Ode
in memoriam William Matthews

You could believe a life so plain it means
calmness in the lives of others, who come
to see it, hold it, buy it piece by piece,
as these good people easing from their van
onto the curb where the big-shoed children
of Charm, Ohio, have lined their baskets
of sweet corn, peaches, green beans, and snap-peas.
Each Saturday morning the meeting point
of many worlds is a market in Charm.

You could believe a name so innocent
it is accurate and without one blade
of irony, and green grass everywhere.
Yet, how human a pleasure the silk hairs
when the corn is peeled back, and the moist worm
curls on the point of an ear like a tongue,
how charged the desire of the children who
want to touch it, taste it, turn it over,
until it has twirled away in the dust.

There are black buggies piled high with fruit pies.
There are field things hand-wrought of applewood
and oak, and oiled at the palm of one man.
There are piecework quilts black-striped and maroon
and mute as dusk, and tatting, and snow shawls,
and cozies the colors of the prize hens–
though the corporate farm five miles away
has made its means of poultry production
faster, chickens fatter, who need no sleep.

Their machinery rumbles the nights through.
Still, it is hard to tell who lives with
more placid curiosity than these,
not only the bearded men in mud boots
and city kids tugging on a goat rope,
but really the whole strange market of Charm,
Ohio, where weekly they come, who stare
and smile at each other, to weigh the short
business end of a dollar in their hands.

J.T. Barbarese

Diorama

Tonight, his fingers on his lips,
his bangs around his brow,
nude except for his black tee shirt,
his white ass radiates,
shines like a plumped peace sign
half in and out of a quilt.
The models of the *Challenger*
and a Hellcat swing from threads
over clothes, books, his rocks and stones.
This is the living theater of all he knows.
All history is still about him.
I adjust his quilt and remember,
tucking his bare ass back in,
a picture of the slaughtered Chinese
of Nanking, in some coffee table book,
of babies, mostly, the backs of their heads
and their diapered or naked white asses
the only human wholes
in all that strewn anatomy.
Outside his window, my back to it,
is the fall's harvest of wet leaves
stuck to his window, the roof below.
I spotted them the moment I entered,
flattened and glued to window and roof,
sleety and white and roundish,
and now that I can't see them,
they are sooty valentines,
they are severed hands waving blurrily,
they are shiny and callipygian
against the cold black tin.

Jim Barnes

The Glass Pyramid

After a long walk down from the Crillon
we enter the arched passage under the Louvre
that leads out to the courtyard where light on

the pyramid shimmers. In line we move
with droves of tourists from the fabled East
toward the depths to view once again the best

things time and corrupting men have left this world.
The Japanese on my left bows and speaks
of Pearl Harbor. I bow and apologize for
Hiroshima. We think we know the peaking
glass cannot fall and we are safe within
this vaulted place where time is stilled and thin

boards and cloth reveal images we want
to engrave forever on our minds. Shadows
of the dead are burned on Nagasaki stone.
These shades on canvas ended, too. We throw
our lives away by not remembering,
the eye's line, the dropped head, the broken ring

of dancers in the field. I look into El
Greco's night and feel the exploding wind
rush and roar down Toledo's cracking hills,
down the ash streets of Hiroshima. The end
of time was always on the old masters' minds.
There is no other reason we can find

to explain the drive artists must have had
to burst the color so that the human
soul shines out like sunlight off foil. A bad
display of contemporary art can't explain
real pain as well as Titian could. We try
to see it all while there is still a time,

and something in us tells us we will not
succeed. Too many lives east and west stand
to fall. Glimpses are all that we can note,
a brief handshake, a bow. No way to explain
the messes of mankind except through art
where once in a while someone gets it right.

Marilyn Bates

Frozen Sperm & Frozen Eggs

My mother and I
from the kitchen table
tune in Oprah. Her
guest is forty, and she's
sparring with her Ex
over frozen sperm.
The audience torpedoes
the ethics professor
who dubs her progeny
"souvenir babies."
They cheer instead
for the grieving couple
who've rented a womb
for their daughter's
frozen egg, an unborn
orphan left behind
in a cancer clash.

"Who'd tell those stories
on themselves?" my mother
asks. She's always had
a husband, blitzed by men
when she was young. She
doesn't understand those
who trade the delicate
whistle of a phallus
for a ghost at the end
of a loveless match.

She doesn't understand
the pathology of Alone.
How it is to be a blank
on the calendar that's
never pencilled in,
a platter of salmon served
to nibbling strangers,
delving in for the center
slice, leaving limes
and fins for the clean-up

crew. How it is to be
a player in some
Broadway version of
Don't Kiss Me Kate, every
actor in his fifteen
minutes of fame, the night
stretched out in an endless
Warhol film, looped to
replay, replay.

"Who'd want a frozen
egg, a frozen sperm?"
my mother asks, swabbing
honey in her cup.
I add lemon to my tea
and say, "We'd do anything
to get that little fuse
that sets the womb
ticking again."

Wendy Battin

The News from Mars

*... the diaspora of human civilization is
bound to go on and out, as it always has done in the process of
setting new frontiers.*
        –Gerard K. O'Neill

1. *Earth*
The sky buzzed as always with its crossing traffic.
Then came the flash, a last photograph
before we disappeared, in negative color:

>   red trees reflected in the orange pond,

>   the roses cool blue holes
>   in the garden's fire,

>   and the cloud, blossoming chastely
>   like an unused sun coming up.

This quiet. This unimagined.
It was a dream stolen from a movie.
Even in sleep I had no other language
for it but film,

the art of light, light's preservation,

and broken from sleep I am
crazy with this fiction.
This morning the world has not ended,
is not transfigured.
Streetlights dim in the gray sky. The garish
dream lights blink out, in room after room
of this city block.

2. *Off-planet: Mars*
The horizon-line clear and arched as an orange.
Above it, blackness with stars, the faint
enormous corkscrew of the galaxy. Below it,
all ground is foreground. Every lazy step
reels more of the world in. Think of

Nijinsky, who told the reporter, *Just leap
into the air, and pause a little.*

Our heads are heavier than our hearts,
as we'd always suspected.

The two moons cross in the sky,
and the doubled shadows merge:

at my feet, then trailing
my drifting body, the black
body of a woman, foreshortened
and sexless in her bulky suit.
My breath is a storm in my helmet, and what
I see, I see through it.

3. *Earth: Night Fallen*
Through my window, with its glass
flowing year after year
into the base of its frame,

Mars is a dull red spot hanging over the warehouse,
and all I imagine about it begins

it is not like this: no rain trapping
the light on the surface of the black street;
no street. The movie must have ended
with the good people helping each other, the bad

looting and double-crossing and dying badly.
The good die well, or stand
brave and elegiac against the ruined backdrop.

Grace Bauer

Flowers in February

Its been so long since I've felt
love, at least the piercing arrow kind,
the sharp stab of passion that enters you
and leaves you feeling changed, though
for three cold nights now I have dreamed
a stranger's presence in my bed, ridden
his eager body into morning, and so
this morning when I find the valentine
a friend, now dead, sent me seven years ago–
a blue acrylic postcard heart captioned:
EXTREMELY DIDACTIC, I laugh less
than I might have once. AIDS got him.
That sickly aftermath of desire some
self-righteous bastards claim is proof
God wants to destroy my friend and *his kind*–
as if they, themselves, were immune to worse
deficiencies of their own. I know I'm not.
Like this love thing. God knows I have
often given it my best shot–*the best years
of my life* some might even say, though the critic
in me would remind them those words have been said
all too often. Maybe calling cliche what it is
is part of my problem, since isn't it
love that often renders us dewy-eyed and speechless,
reliant on chocolates and greeting cards
to get our point across? Perhaps we should
remind ourselves the original Valentine
was a saint, some guy who probably resisted
getting laid on grounds of faith. I have
no such grounds to stand on, just my own
unsaintly failures: a deficit of beauty
or character, a history of wanting men
who didn't want back, till after years
of this I've come to find an uneasy safety

in avoiding desire, settling for solitude.
Still there are these flowers everywhere
which make one want to reconsider, and strangers
at parties with a glint in their eyes that insists
them into your dreams. There are the cards
you've kept for years to remind you that even
dead men made you laugh once, and so you
approach your mailbox hoping for something
hidden between the rejections and overdue
bills, some bleeding cardboard heart to give
your own heart more reason for beating.

Marvin Bell

Sounds of the Resurrected Dead Man's Footsteps #3

1. *Beast, Peach and Dance*
He couldn't say it or write it or sign it or give it a name.
He was suffering, he was terrible, he had a shape you could see in the fire.
He blamed the wine, God, the infamous events of Bethlehem.
Each newborn appeared to him in the air, their gorgeous proportions
    shaping the swaddling cloth each to each.
On the one hand, he felt the galaxies cooling, the gears clogging and the old
    passions frozen into debilitating poses.
On the other hand, it was now April and he had a buzz on because some
    seasons are their own nectar.
He could pick out a jacket and tie if he had to.
He could sit without twitching through the outdoor Mozart, the band shell
    gleaming like a new star.
Around him, the concert-goers sat tight-lipped, their expectations
    rewarded.
Before him, the night took on the sheen of flat glass and he could see in it
    the beacons of the town, and the blue-blackness of space just beyond.
His eyes fixed on a small, fuzzy star among many larger stars.
He became obsessed with this star, certain it was a Jewish star.
He felt that, if he could follow it, it would lead him to the true story
    of Jesus.
That night, while Mozart resolved in the air, he began to travel through
    time.
His small star would someday pass close to him but not yet.

2. *Angel, Portrait and Breath*
The hands that were nailed, the ankles that were pierced as if one–he had seen such proclamations before, it being common.
The bodies that literally came unglued in the furnace, the bones festering in lye–he had seen the piles of coats and eyeglasses, there being many.
The same angel who watched over the crucified Jesus passed over the cremated Jews, or was that a cloud?
The smokestacks carried away their last breaths.
Then Jesus rose entire to show the power of belief.
The dead Jews disintegrated into earth, air and water to show the lasting effects of evil.
He could not give it a name but felt that night as if, whatever it was, it lived on a small star, encircled but apart.
Thereafter, ordinary objects displayed a consciousness of the presence of men and women.
The blackened pots and ladles of the kitchen appeared changed.
They shone from long years of sustenance, from soups and sauces.
And in the shop he felt it also in the saws and sawhorses, in the dropcloths and bent nails, each encrusted with the years.
In this manner, he came to see in common objects the shine of the angelic.
The divine and horrific were linked by things and their descendants.
It was possible to see the good and bad in a needle and thread, in a pencil and pad, in a spoon, in a shoe.
The cloud appeared to him by day and the little star by night.

Sounds of the Resurrected Dead Man's Footsteps #6

1. *Skulls*
Oh, said a piece of tree bark in the wind, and the night froze.
One could not have foreseen the stoppage.
I did not foresee it, who had expected a messiah.
No one had yet dared say that he or she was it–target or savior.
In the slippage between time and the turning planet, a buildup of dirty grease made movement difficult.
Time slowed down while events accelerated.
The slower the eye moved, the faster events went past.
The raping and pillaging over time became one unending moment.
Nazis, who would always stand for the crimes of culture, clustered in public intersections, awaiting deliveries.
The masses would turn in the Jews.
From the officers' quarters could be heard the beautiful Schubert.
And in the camp there was the grieving tenor of the cantor.

The one rose and the other sank.
Today, one can stroll in the footsteps of those who walked single file from this life.
Often I stand in the yard at night expecting something.
Something in the breeze one caught a scent of as if a head of hair had passed by without a face.
Whatever happens to us from now on, it will come up from the earth.
It will bear the grief of the exterminated, it will lug itself upwards.
It will take all of our trucks to carry the bones.
But the profane tattoos have been bled of their blue by the watery loam, additives for worms.
Often I stand in the yard with a shovel.

2. *Skulls*
I am the poet of skulls without why or wherefore.
I didn't ask to be this or that, one way or another, just a young man of words.
Words that grew in sandy soil, words that fit scrub trees and beach grass.
Sentenced to work alone where there is often no one to talk to.
The poetry of skulls demands complicity of the reader, that the reader put words in the skull's mouth.
The reader must put water and beer in the mouth, and music in the ears, and fan the air for aromas to enter the nostrils.
The reader must take these lost heads to heart.
The reader must see with the eyes of a skull, comb the missing hair of the skull, brush the absent teeth, kiss the lips and find the hinge of the tongue.
Yes, like Hamlet, the Jew of Denmark before Shakespeare seduced him.
It is the things of the world which rescue us from the degradations of the literati.
A workshirt hanging from a nail may be all the honesty we can handle.
I am beloved of my hat and coat, enamored of my bed, my troth renewed each night that my head makes its impression on the pillow.
I am the true paramour of my past, though my wife swoons at the snapshots.
Small syringe the doctor left behind to charm the child.
Colorful *yarmulke* that lifted the High Holy Days.

Sounds of the Resurrected Dead Man's Footsteps #13

1. *Millennium*
Like trying to pour entropy through a funnel.
The devilish moment, the thought that a ceremony might make of one second something so illuminating it would forever define us.
The illusion that a hand holding another hand is attached to it.
Nothing I say or do.
This here means right now, rigorous as it is to be here now, not there then.
One respects Miss Stein for avoiding the future.
Then there is the flashbulb that gets in one's eyes.
The mercury ascends in the thermometer, then bumps on down.
Where were you when the world changed?
In southern Australia where the time zone was half-an-hour ahead.
Thus, poetry without reference to time: *i.e.*, he has an artificial heart but he still feels love.
Poetry regional within the body.
The mind always half-an-hour behind.
A sundial cannot be read under a Bo tree.
Your hand in mine on the midnight in question crystallized the moment, or was it tears?

2. *Posterity*
The all-inclusive later, after you have read the piece about now.
After the bawling is over, beyond contretemps, past knowledge of mishaps.
Then's beyond.
But you want to know ahead of time–does she, will I, will it keep?
Or not.
Throws a stone at a tree and, if it hits, the best is yet to be.
Throws a stone at a tree and, if it misses, throws another.
Did you act out such childhood rituals also?
Draws a line in the dirt before he beheads the chicken.
Keeps an umbrella in the car so it won't rain.
Recognition of hazards and safe areas.
Careful with mirrors, shies from reflective surfaces, smiles at the camera.
A catalog of traits, survival skills, mannerisms and customs, a complete list of instinctual responses and reflexes, an inventory of do's and don'ts.
Nothing left to chance in the attempt to influence posterity.
That is, nothingness is left to chance, the chips fall where they may, and the outcome remains unknown.
Quantum mechanics: a new generation redefines normalcy.
The seers rewinding their watches, the clairvoyants squinting.

Shuffling the Tarot, recasting the *I Ching*, wrinkling the lifeline, envisioning
    happenstance, charting chaos, counting butterflies.
The new scythe swinging through poetry may or may not have been honed.
My goal to be better than dirt.

Joe David Bellamy

Light Years

The new galaxies are billions of light years away, so we
only see the way they were billions of years ago. The
farther away we look into the universe, the farther we see
into the past of the universe. If galaxies are ten billion
light years from Earth, we see them as they were ten billion
years ago. They could be utterly dead, an absence in space,
and we wouldn't know about it for ten billion years! But
then in ten billion years, we might not be here to see it.

If we could get far enough away from Earth and still see it,
we would be able to see into our own pasts. In order to see
fifty years into the past, we would have to be located today
at a distance of fifty light years from Earth. But getting
to that distance would take us fifty years, even if we could
travel at the speed of light and by the time we got there
(even if we could travel at the speed of light) we would
only be seeing our own departure, not into the past.

A billion years from now, the light of this day will be
received and seen by creatures who live at a distance of
one billion light years from Earth—a form of immortality.
The light of every moment we have lived is traveling now
out across the universe. Light, once emitted, goes on forever.
A moment, once lived, is indelibly written in light and
projected irretrievably across the face of the universe.

Don Bogen

Among Appliances

They are so busy and self-involved as I hear them muttering in the distance
that they strike me sometimes as sheer marvels:
the dishwasher filling its huge blue gullet—a cluck from the timer,
and spindly wings spew out scalding water in the dark—

or its basement cousin chugging yet another load through the changes,
whirling, rocking, belching gray suds and lint into the concrete washtubs.

Though I can never keep track of them all, I'm charmed by the cycles:
their varied lengths, sudden shifts and rigorous sense of time,
the control knob simple as a windup clock, language of click and whir,
mysterious pauses while something is draining or filling,
or silence even while something is gathering strength.
There's a music in these risings and fallings–odd rest, crescendo,
    diminuendo–
the soothing predictable pattern of potential and release.

I am no technophile, not all machines give this comfort.
Our vacuum cleaner is a ball and chain that growls as you try to make it
    work,
I have never wanted a yard big enough to need a power mower,
and lamps I have always thought of as most useful when unnoticed
like a perfectly attendant butler wearing a small hat.

I like the ones that have their own intricate lives–
not too private or powerful, like the bank machine that calls you by name
    and suddenly gulps your card,
nothing fussy or intimidating, nothing imitating a person,
but the stolid non-interactive types that work for years, supporting the
    whole household:
the refrigerator shuddering to keep cold then deciding–who knows
    when?–to defrost itself,
the furnace drumming up flames, beating a hot breeze through the frilly
    cast iron vents,
the dryer tumbling socks and lingerie in a blurred luxurious jumble.
All these big boxes with their timers and thermostats,
defining the stages of their tasks, devouring what I feed them,
pulling the current up through the basement meter.

It is shameful but sometimes I want them all on.
I set the controls and leave, like an absent deist god,
but am also content to work among them with a broom or sponge for a
    time,
a robot master tidying up around laborious metal lives.

Harold Bond

Living with Pain

At the outset you try
to destroy it by any means
you can, miscalculating
the awesomeness of its power.
When you realize
the futility of your efforts,
you bite your lip and drop
your fists in resignation
to its will. There are times
you are convinced it means you
no harm, that its one duty
in life is to remind you
you are mortal. Then it goes
shooting through you again
with such relentlessness
that you know it can never
have your best interests at heart.
There are times you pretend
it is not there and focus
instead on all the good things
in your life, but the charade
brings you no relief. You try
to pacify it with gum drops,
hoping it has a sweet tooth.
You tell stories to it, hoping
it will sleep and not wake up.
It curries favors from no one.
It is always precisely itself.
Finally, you drop to your knees
before it like a lover.
You introduce it to your wife.
You pull up a chair for it
at the dinner table.
You offer it your bathrobe
and favorite slippers and whatever
else it desires. You know
now it means to be a part of you
for all the rest of your days.

Philip Booth

Late Wakings

This is the gray of it.
                    Even the house.
All its everythings so much nothing.
Far from what we believed it once meant.
Every mail tries to sell elsewhere: offers
of off-season discounts, countless folders
of equatorial beaches, condos, and sun.
Here the gales, steely weathers, sleet.
Aside from the sun, nothing we've longed for.
Predators overhead, hawks dying to stoop.
Scavenging gulls, ravens, working the street.
Everywhere, where we apparently live, fear.
Anger on narrowing edges. We wake from nightmares
to nightmare newscasts. So it's morning again,
again.
        All day the sky's smearing up.

Perry Brass

Two San Francisco Poems

Seven P.M. in San Francisco
It is seven P.M. in San Francisco,
at the corner of Church and Market,
and I am sitting in a fast-food joint
that serves pieces of roast chicken
and despite the grind of sameness
that chases each man away
from the moment, the air seems
to hum with possibilities,
with action, desire, excitement.
And the giddy lights of traffic
are streaming, dream-like, in front of me,
and young men are scurrying
up and down, on the way to this
and that and are thinking about tomorrow,
because it's going to be

so different from today. While fear
for a moment seems to have cleared
the night, early as it is, dropping on us
hope like money in the bank, in the form
of time that we can dance to
and enjoy all the way to Sunday.
It is Saturday night and early,
and we're in this pleasurable city
of streetcars and hills and views;
and the sea way, way out there,
all beckoning and salty and clear–
like the air, does not inspire fear
tonight, but only temptations of delight:
all there in San Francisco
on a warm, early fall Saturday night.

Nov. 8, 1997

The Poets Do Not Sing Songs Anymore
The poets do not sing songs anymore–
our voices have been muted,
have been diluted by stupidity
and commerce and do not spring
from us like nightingales
or the tenor cry of larks
on suicidal flights
to bring back morning heat to their wings.
The poets do not sing
this way–natural–open throated.
Fresh, brave, in love.
We have become duped and sorrowful,
in debt to dull adulthood. We do not sing
like children, or homosexual troubadours
or painted French courtiers
in consort with Apollo
chasing Hyacinth through marsh lands,
chasing love's own cornered scream
that settles like violet ribbons
from a distant mountain, slowly spilling
arabesques and ginger curls
of light upon itself: we poets
do not sing of this, and my heart
suffers in its absence.

Nov. 8, 1997

Debra Bruce

Follow-up Exam

Only when I lift both arms above
my head, as when a child is asked *How big?*
and reaches high and solemnly and waits
to be released by whoops of praise; and only

since that long girlhood of mine is long
gone, my hospital gown open, as I hold
this pose at your request so your hand can guide
their gaze across my breasts; and even then

only these discerning interns would notice
my subtle loss of shape, last summer's scar.
As far as anyone can tell, the wish
my well-wishers had for me to push beyond

the unspeakable news you gave one year ago
is granted. They call my name each time I turn
to look away as if I'd heard a voice
behind a screen at dusk. I must return

to you each season, to your hands' brisk passage
across my flesh, each nipple rubbed for no one's
pleasure, in pure thought, and finally,
your findings. I make my well-trained terror wait

for you to give permission not yours to give
which I grab from you each time you shake my hand
and let me go. As far as anyone knows,
even you, we'll meet again when pears are long

since fallen, soft, scuffed. I'm off
for now. I'm on my feet, outside, out there
where all the others seem to be, where another
brazen summer noon is holding forth.

Joseph Bruchac

Men of the Forest

In the Hanover Zoo
    in Germany,
the orang-utan,
      whose name in Malay
          means "Man of the Forest,"
shambles over
    to the thick plate glass
        answering the signs
           I make with my hands.
Brother
    I see you
        Our Creator
           made both our spirits free

Its eyes
    hold questions
    an elder might ask
        of a child.

So my old people,
    men of the forest,
      were brought to this Europe
        put on exhibit,
      seen as less
          than human.

We hold our hands up
    palm to palm
        feeling the warmth
           of ancestry
              pass
                  through the centuries
                  and the vanished glass.

Christopher Buckley

Opera
in memoriam Bill Matthews

Up-graded from economy class, I'm flying down the freeway
feeling rich as God, behind the wheel of a silver, full-size
sedan—quad stereo, cruise control, gold glowing digital clock.
For a minute I recall that article on the Sultan of Brunei
checking out from a hotel and leaving enough money in tips
to fund disease research for a year. But soon I'm satisfied
just floating through a corridor of pines, popping in my tape
of Carerras, Domingo, and Pavarotti. A chorus of blue above me,
a few arpeggios of clouds to the right, not unlike the sky
over the Baths of Caracalla where they're singing—three ancient
stories of brick still standing on the edge of Rome. We came
across it one summer as workers were erecting the stage
and high dusty towers for *Aida*—40 then, and just beginning
to listen....
        70 mph and I'm transported by the wind-
swell of the orchestra, lifted by the violins, brought back
to earth by violoncellos, the heart still climbing that white
ladder of hope with "Rondine al Nido," Pavarotti's power
surge spiking current along my arms. I let the tape rewind—
this is serious, I keep hearing, we are all going to die,
hopelessly though, and at last in love with the world.
By now, most my aspirations let go, blown by me like litter
along the road, I'm just happy to be breathing, to be soaring
in such company, to have a heart thumping its own sprung notes.

No one is going to sleep until Pavarotti has an answer
to the riddle and claims the starry heart of Turandot—
now all three encore "Nessun Dorma," and in the bridge
all the angels sing, sodality in the last movement of lost air.
I too want to fly, to know the ineluctable extravagance
of the spirit about to slip out of the tux, beyond the fingertips
into the night sky.
        But I have to rent a car to hear
these tapes punched up to the proper brick-shaking valence.
I have to leave town, get away from young friends at parties
where the angels all wear red shoes, where I'm told Dwight Yoakam
is "Bakersfield Opera," where CDs are stacked like potato chips—
either trash bands like Pilonidal Cyst, Meat Puppets, and

Mud Honey, or time fractures from the 70s, Hendrix, Led Zeppelin,
and the Chambers Brothers. Nothing close to carrying off the sky
like Verdi or Puccini–in heaven, they have to be cooking Italian!

Friends my age are all listening to opera–Pavarotti's Richter Scale
and range proving there's another level, and though the register,
like the body, is giving way to gravity, there is something
there just above us.
                The astral body must be like this,
all sentience and incorporeal as sound. I want some singing
about that–all the red and blue bright threads spun out
from our hearts, spooled above the gilt-edged clouds,
above the scraps of flesh and diminuendos of ordinary time.
I want this feeling of atoms falling out of the crystal orbits
of the earth, yet reclaimed by arias, by cavatinas.
Carrerras recovering from cancer, Domingo's good looks
going south, Pavarotti barely able to move–yet each lifting
past the burning limits of the dark. And conducting everything,
Zubin Mehta–surely that has to be an angel's name?
But this is serious, we are all going to die.

Andrea Hollander Budy

The Hunters

Dressed in their green spotted drabs to blend in
with trees, my father and his new friends, then
nineteen, erected their dark tents and dug
a latrine, then gathered twigs from the edge

of their camp and the driest leaves, and at
twilight all of them assembled, then bent
their heads for a moment over their Tang
or their coffee or tea, and one boy sang

a little prayer in the unarmed quiet
(at night sometimes my father still sings it),
and even the air began to settle
except for the occasional rattle

of insects and in the nearby distance
mortar fire from Da Nang, insistent.

Grace Butcher

The Last War

The deer stand in driveways,
back yards, parking lots,
waiting to be shot.
We *have* to shoot them;
they are killing us.
They jump onto our bumpers,
leap through our windshields,
tangle with our tires.

When two populations
are in each other's way,
they kill each other.
That's just how it is.

We wear their coats;
they eat our corn.
We stalk them in woods and fields;
they lie in wait alongside the roads.
They bother us with their beauty;
we harden ourselves against it.
They breakfast on the bark
of our young apple trees
and help themselves to our vegetables.
We ambush them from high in the trees
and hang car hats on their antlers.
We build our houses in their front yards.
They wander our lawns in the moonlight.
No one needs their statues now;
we have the real thing.

We should put out birth control pills
among the corn, do the same for ourselves.
Love, lust–they are what they are.
Neither side is going to give in, go away.
If they did leave, we'd follow them,
hunt them anyhow even though
we're well fed, well clothed.
Something in our blood
tells us to do it.
That's just how we are.

If we left, they'd find us again,
filter in among us, always at dusk,
to wait for our new gardens to grow.
They'd be like ghosts, haunting us.
It would take a long time
for us to realize they were there again
waiting for us to die, waiting for the woods
to close in and cover everything,
the way it used to be,
before the war.

Lucas Carpenter

ByeByeBlackbird
in memoriam Miles Davis

In a broken-down Charleston dive, The Brick,
where the late folks gathered after all else failed,
this was the hot jukebox punch the winter
I flew south for the geographical cure.
The first time Miles cut his muted way through to me
I was embalmed in a 3 A.M. smoky aspic
that seemed to jiggle when I shifted my barstool perch
to light a smoke or raise my glass. Carl
had opened the back door (as was his wont)
to clear the air before dawn's closing
with the first stirrings of morning breeze
from the harbor and the ocean beyond.
I took it full in the face: the briny cool
admitting Miles at the beginning of this tune.

Years later I'm still amazed
how he lays out on the refrain,
letting the rhythm go on alone.
You still hear what is not there
because you know it should be
and he knows you know.

At Lincoln Center he turned his back,
walking to the rear of the stage,
playing to a blank wall.
The audience was left to overhear,
some ill-at-ease, others angry.

Yet if they surrendered to him,
let him work his way, they
heard a purer Miles, his sound
without his face, bringing them
beyond the melody he'd left behind.
Only his music mattered then,
but more than music happened in that room.

When I saw him outside at Montreux,
he sent ice-blue abstractions over acres of crowd,
out to where music has no name.
I tried to meet him backstage afterwards,
dodging security to get close enough
to shout his name. He
turned his head towards me
when he heard it.

Hayden Carruth

Small Fundamental Essay

What many people fail to understand
about the art and science of mechanics
is that you may know perfectly what happens
under the hood of your car when you turn on
the ignition, and you may comprehend
to a nicety how the combination of pump
and pressure tank and heating coils produces
hot water when you turn the tap, and yet
the wonder never ceases. That this can be
–and is–is what bestirs the mind and heart.
Is this a faith? It never starts a war
nor rips a seam out of a living city,
it needs no ghastly hierophant hung up
dead on a cross to speak for us. But yes,
it is a faith. Faith in the miracle of the
possible, in the peaceful knowledge of what is true.

Turner Cassity

Performing *Le Prophète,*
or,
Meyerbeer in Texas

To Waco as to Münster John of Leyden
Comes, accompanied again by arms
And charges of conducting orgies. Few
Cults, fewer orthodoxies, can avert
The joint mind-set of siege. Compound denotes
Two elements as well as guards and walls.
A prophet is with honor in such lands
As he controls, allowing therefore church
Or state to prophesy, although a state
Calls prophecies "projections." Shows of force,
And force's foretold actuality,
The rams move in; the tanks are battering.
They and their times are interchangeable.
And, orange on the dingy desert flats,
The gasoline leaps up: a tongue of flame
At once flamethrower, purge, and Pentecost.
On Baptist turf the Anabaptist burn.

Michael Castro

Chili Mac
for Allen Ginsberg

Poets want Irv's Good Food
not because of the sight rhyme
but because this is a real diner, white tiled exterior
& spinning counter stools–
the last of a dying breed in South St. Louis.
Greasy menus, Nehru capped cook, lone gray waitress,
derelicts mingling with investment brokers–
all bow
to your egalitarian fare.

A genuine place. Bus stop waiters
get invited in out of the cold.
Everyone knows everyone–if you're new
you're soon known. No need

to introduce yourself.
The gruff staff will name you. Ginsberg
came in & tried the Chili-Mac Special,
grilled the cook about how to make it, for who,
& why. Is it popular? The interrogation
went on & on.
It all boiled down
to three words.

Cheap and Filling.
Allen looked at me.
Like good poetry, we thought. More
for less.
We ordered some & it filled the bill.
More American than apple pie.
Yankee Doodle's Italian pasta,
the feather in his cap,
tickling Native American beans & peppers.
Multi-cultural dialogue afloat
in the gastric juices.
Irv asked, *Is it good?*

It was a good year
before I needed to go back.
Allen long gone from Burroughs' home town.

I walked in the door & was greeted like a regular.
Howyadoin Bud? said the chef.
Well, well, well. Mr. Budget. chimed in the waitress.
Where's Mac? the chef asked.
I looked at him weird.
You know,
your friend with the beard, he said.
Chili-Mac.

Ed Chaberek

The American
He was 23 at Wounded Knee. Made his stand
alongside others that fell. Bullets missed–
barely. Went to hell inside a booze
bottle. Woke up in this world. Wondered
why. "Too dumb to die, I guess." Did

it all–60s, 70s. Vietnam Vet. Mad
as hell. Indian but with a very white
ancestor: "Way back... we all have our
skeletons." Back to college. Gave up drink. Now
enters rooms, others step aside. "Scare
'um... educated Injun. Ugh." Chuckles. Been
in a hundred sweats, done the Sun Dance, re-
treated to the hard Montana hills. Nearly
died–for real. Forty days–no food. Came
back. "All the scales fell. How they fell. Ate
a rattler to break my fast, returned
God coiled tightly in my heart."

James Wm. Chichetto

Blind Veteran (Korean War)

He can tell where he is by the echo on the lake,
    his paddles brushing against pickerelweed,
the air giving him its own path over the entire water.

He talks of battle, of those long dead
    far beyond the hearing of other ears
        browsing one summer at dawn—
        each soldier taking a step forward
            until something happened,
    and across their clothes blood had grown
        out of all they had done.

He calls out to my aunt at dusk,
    above the heads of birds, above shore
        fowl and land far back into the rocks,
    and she calls back to him from a small wharf,
She'll holler him back to shore.

Paul Christensen

Ode to Dolly

To escape the womb, that is the question.
Whether it is wiser to make life
from our hands, a little brain work,
some doodles on the scratch pad,

a theory of cell genesis, or accede
to something else's will–this female
dominion over life, this underworld
of eggs ruled by Demeter's harrow,
poses our dilemma. Now Dolly shivers
and stands up in her chemical stall,
purified of germs, a clone without
variety, snout-heavy, dumb-eyed creature.

Take Descartes' paranoia, Bacon's
essential quarrel with the natural,
a history of witch burnings, an assault
upon the alchemists, some desire
to end the last connection between
the placental earth and this homunculus
of pride, and *hello Dolly!*
She is our Trojan sheep, her belly
meaningless, her womb an attic
in the body. Just hocks and hams,
a butcher shop of side meats and organs,
a commodity without the ewe's milk
to give it heritage. She stands as if
cut out by Matisse's small arthritic hand,
set out against a black construction
of abandoned nature. What next? A bullcalf
carved from leg cells, stirred into a
pregnant cocktail, poured out upon
a satin pasture. Oh Dolly, oh plastic
replica, little squeeze-toy with a cry
on loop tape, eyes hinged to your wooden
head, your mouth a Hans Bellmer grin
of malice, thou contraption, thou
Futurist utope and genetic yo-yo.

Mengele had a little lamb,
little lamb, little lamb!
Mengele had a little lamb
whose fleece was white as snow.

African Elegy

In west Africa, the e-coli bacteria
is nothing to the AIDS gnawing at the center;
in Rwanda the Hutu have learned
to kill more quickly, without the paperwork.
The Tutsi are expert at reprisal,
and in the camps the murderers eat first.
In Angola, the land's outcrop is a freighter port
for oil and contraband, and the heavies
have been killing over it for decades.

Listen. It's the first wind of the rainy season.
It comes over the red powder like a ghost,
darkening noon. The streets go pink
with whirs, and the trees, limp and
punctured by bats, flap like old women.
A man sleeps in the shadow of a death house.

The water in the ditch is for drinking,
and the boys with round, drum-tight bellies
scoop their pots above the gray silt.
The smell of taro meal rises out of thatch
to mix with the bitterness. A pepper burns
unattended in the skillet. Someone pukes
blood into his palms and wipes the strings
from his mouth. He will not be hungry.

Lie down with me, Africa, and be still.
The only danger is resentment, anger.
The ruins are all a western diary of greed
written in your blood, your wandering spirits.
The mock-nations evaporate like shadows
from the map. This violence, this mayhem
of Lagos and Mogadishu, the Congo
of blood cascading like Victoria Falls
upon the future, is all a consequence
beyond repair. Let it occur without remorse,
and lay fresh straw, prepare for birth.

David Citino

Ode to Billie Dove
One of the most beautiful stars of silent film...
          –The New York Times

And now she's become one
of the most silent stars of film.
She was 97, lived in
the retirement community
of the Motion Picture and Television Fund

with hundreds of others trying
to recall their marks, their cues.
Damsel in distress, her speciality.
Through reels and reels,
Black Pirate, Night Watch, Stolen Bride,

she'd roll her eyes and feign fear
enough to rouse the beast
in every manly breast, so that,
if thoughts could be heard–as
sometimes they are on stage–

theaters would resound with vows,
I'll save you, Billie Dove!
Quaint, this may seem now,
but how hurtful it has always been,
millennia of the fear, coyness, guile

a woman is forced to practice
to make her way with men.
Scenes produced, directed by him.
Still today it sells big time–
the cellar sound she must investigate,

the chase through woods in heels,
or, with moon-pale decolletage,
up from bed to remove the crucifix,
open the window to the squeak,
the flap of undying thirst.

O Billie, you've no need to put
yourself in harm's way now.
You've earned equal billing

with the male lead, a part as large.
Roles are no better today

than seventy years ago, but
now, forever above you
on the door shining bright
as polished marble, a sign
pointing to that far fairer place–

we hope–you have your star.

DeWitt Clinton

Touring the Holocaust

We load politely
into yellow buses,
whisk across town
a few already queasy
nearly all of us wear
pink triangles, others
hold special passes
in the back one old woman
starts weeping.

At the entrance
a guide tells us
we have precisely two hours
so we should move quickly
or we will miss
the final part
the part everyone
has heard about
the part no one can miss.

Car load by car load
ascends to the top
spellbound by what
a young sergeant says
a pile so high
it could not be
what looks like human pyramids
suddenly the doors open
all of us push

to get out some already
weeping before we even
get to the part
the part everyone
has heard about
the part no one can miss
we stare into
blow ups   Army photographs
how impossible
to distinguish
Reuben from Marla from Maurice.

Even the guards up here
look different
as if they already
know what is at the end
no matter how quick
we walk, no matter....
We cannot move any further
unless we step
into a car
a brown cattle car
swept incredibly clean
where all of us must
unload nothing bad will happen
to us here
though we cannot stay
too long in the car
that would bring the guards
everyone believes
we will be safe
it isn't as if
we are really there.

In the next hall
we lose sight
slow down
as waves of choking
close our eyes
all around us
a constant weeping
remembering

the guide warns us
to keep walking this way
"it won't do any good
to stop here
please remember we close
in an hour, please move along"

dazed, disoriented, we step
into a *shtetl* sky high
a room of old photos
of everyone who ever
lived in that place
this fire place
high as a smokestack
those at the very top
lift first into ash.

In the next room
children who walk through
may not look over the wall
that keeps them from seeing
what so mesmerizes
those just arriving
want to see what draws
a crowd like this
doctors circling
the almost living
pushed beyond the howls
of patient and knife.

Finally we approach
the krematorium
a model of long courteous lines
little people with
little faces
guards and shepherds
keeping everyone
civil, in line

we watch them go inside
watch the innocent undress
the inappropriateness
of men and women

long beards
pubic hair
a wildness beyond even G-d
how everyone fits in
packed, compressed,
up on the roof,
in miniature
an officer drops a pellet
of Zyklon-B
in the next building
we see ovens
the Allies would not bomb
a constant baking
of Jews, Gypsies, dwarves,
cripples, homosexuals, the insane,
all those bodies lifted up to G-d
a plume
we cannot forget.

The loudspeaker
reminds us
closing time
is in 30 minutes
on our way past
the packed furnaces
we pause in front of shoes,
shoes of all
kinds a hillside of shoes.

The final rooms
take us out of the camps
into the streets
of Jerusalem, the shouts of joy
rifles popping Jews and Arabs
find a new State
with each other
only 15 minutes remain
we cram into the bookstore
fill our arms
with all we can afford
pretend we have dreamed
we are starved, ravenous,

we skip the bus
so damn lucky
among the few
to walk through
like this
on opening day.

Carole Cohen

Approaching the Internet

Both hands on the keyboard,
an eye on the spell-checking tool, I wonder
what one should wear when entering
a chat room. I am only clothed
in the English language, and that alone
seems a bit revealing. If I enter
and say nothing, just listen
to the conversation, will the others
notice me, know I am there in the dark, *lurking,*
or does some computer blip, some bit of light,
alert them to intruders? Will they like my dress?

I listen, watch, as lines of conversation
burst across the screen, emotions dotted
with punctuation, thoughts in straight lines.
Language shivers under the light blanket
of the paragraph. I can be anyone
in my language, my verbs can nibble
at the ears of my subjects, I can unbutton
my adjectives, stripping them off
slowly, right down to the bare nouns.
Here, I am my best use of language,
no lawyers protect me, no photograph
misrepresents, no birth name, no history,
just the present, the future tenses.
I type *I am,* and I *become.*

My words don't jumble up on the keyboard
as they do in real life. I am shy in the light,
I am not in the dark. *I am, I am.*
In this chat room, I am articulate,
I have a right to have an opinion, my opinion

is, I am heard, I am black today, white tomorrow,
my name *is,* I am rich, poor, live in the city,
the country, I am good, I am bad, *I am*
whatever I want to be that day, represented
only by the alphabet and my computer brain,
by words I choose from a thesaurus,
spell-checked by a computer chip,
I am literate and confident and liberated.

Honesty becomes a first name I use sometimes,
my age is just a figure of speech, my gods
are numerous and convenient, in this
chat room *I am* whatever you want me to be.
In this life in cyberspace, I float around the room,
looking good, thinner than I've ever been,
just making conversation.

Phyllis K Collier

Vanishing

Vanishings are needful,
as silence is to music.
 –Denise Levertov
 1923-1997

In late December's dusk I think of snowflakes
Falling on crumbling basalt hardnosed granite,
Alabaster shudder of feathers alighting
In a ruffle of wings, your words, like music,
Different from any other art, and designed
To set my bones trembling:
Rock   Web   Salamander.
Vaporous barrier reefs, tainted lakes,
A spider inching across a desert,
Palm tree in its vigil where old rocks
Go out to sun themselves,
Conversation of the hills
Revealing a pattern, the intricate way
Threads spool out, where you turned
And looked, eastward to streetlamps
Darkening at dawn. You were the peninsula
Out into the water ahead of the rest of us
To seine the filmy lies, voices in the ground,

Earth devouring the folded cloth. You stepped
Again and again through the glass to find,
One time blood trailing in the rivers,
Another the nuclear hum of the Pacific. Now
Even the hardy milfoil and mullein wilt
Alongside the road. Tiny peals of coral bells
Long silenced lift to you who saw
In the summer bones of the mountain
What could withstand the ravages.

Robert Cording

Dust

Now when priests and faithful say the words
life eternal no representations appear at all.
—Czeslaw Milosz

Not John's new Jerusalem rising out of Babylon,
its whore become a bride newly clothed in light;
not that city's gold brighter than the sun
where one timeless day banished the night

and a branching tree flourished beside a river,
its ripe, healing fruit extended to those
who sing the word's music on both sides of the water
without memory of lives that came to a close.

Not Dante's wheeling rose of ingathering light,
its perfection of form calling us from wandering,
from out days of earthly exile and imperfect sight,
each returning step a remembrance and forgetting.

Nor Luca Signorelli's vision of muscled eloquence,
death's skeletal body given its resurrection
in the perfect symmetry and quick intelligence
of human form leonine in its new dominion.

Not even Keats' earthly paradise of a *finer tone*,
time set aside in the sun's afternoon contemplation
of a bowl of tranquil blue grapes, each misted one
breathing in the light's final satisfaction.

No, we're finally certain that every revelation
is the result of circumstance and need–as today
on CNN, when callers tied up lines at the station

to say they saw Christ himself in the star-ridden gray

photographs sent down by the Hubble telescope. The face
of Gene Shallit came to others. Or the Statue of Liberty.
The *heavens?*–vast yet mappable stretches of space
where we monitor the accidental birth of some new galaxy

or posit a star's dark collapse amidst dark matter.
Where nothing exists because there is no observer.
Now, at odd moments, we feel the terror of dust's
new meaning: there is, of course, nothing more than us.

David Curtis

Feeling

       is the bleat
of cloned or uncloned sheep;
the gurgling of fumaroles–
the Painted Pot–
expresses, too, though what's expressed is not
so clear, yet the poles

of ejaculate sound
and poetry are. This garden is renowned
neither for its profusion
nor variety of roses, merely,
but because that rose was placed over against that tree.
Ordering is fun

and needn't be feared;
still, celebrated passions reared
near superstition's nave
bespecter night.
Science, art's duplicate form, mainly gets it right,
at least up to the grave.

Philip Dacey

Disney: The Wall

The Proposed Disney American History Theme Park "would be split into nine 'playlands' with themes that include... the wrenching era of the Vietnam War."
        —New York Times, June 15, 1994

I'll never forget the way Snow White
stood out so pretty against the polished black
granite and how I jumped when the sniper's shot

stained her gown with fake blood that looked
so real—you can count on the magic of Disney—
I thought I was going to be sick.

Instead I cheered when, slumped against stone, she
launched a flare and the prince looking handsome in
fatigues and combat boots dropped from a Huey

to kill the sniper, who turned out to be the Evil Queen
from Hanoi. And all the dwarves lined along
the top of the wall danced up and down,

even Dopey, who was got up like a Viet Cong
in black silk pajamas I wouldn't mind having a pair of,
when the prince and Snow White exchanged rings

in front of the dates 1959 to 1975
to show us what those war years
were really about—true and undying love.

I cried, but you should have seen the tears
fall when guess who announced that everyone
on the wall was now an honorary mouseketeer—

Mickey himself. He even handed out to each veteran
present a pair of the cutest mouse-ears.
I helped one man with one arm put his on.

It's true he and some of the other vets (hair
short, Walt's rule) freaked when Donald Duck
yelling *Napalm!* threw volleys of water

balloons at them, but I don't think
that little dickens meant anything but good.
Anyway, Donald scrammed when the Buddhist monks

set themselves on fire (college kids
zipped into special suits) for the grand finale
and formed a circle to represent the woods

inside which a starlet playing Bambi
(fluffy tail, and the deer's name sewn
on her tank top) struggled on hands and knees

until a pack of Dalmatians with green
berets tied to their heads rushed in and led her out
to safety in a demilitarized zone,

leaving a ranger to proclaim the end of Tet
as the National Park Service's sprinkler system
put out the monks. Some packs of cigarettes

(gifts left for buddies who didn't come home)
got wet, but the overall point was that war,
even a lost one, can become a good dream

when an entire nation wishes upon a star.
I didn't know a simple wall could be such fun,
and I'm proud that we placed our history

in the hands of the Disney Corporation:
the most American thing we could have done.

On a Contributor's Note for William Stafford
(Cream City Review, Volume 20, Numbers I & 2*)*

He passed away in 1993
was what the note said,
and I knew Stafford hadn't written it,
not because he couldn't have
but because he'd never have said,
except to quote
or maybe dip into the Missouri,
passed away.

He died and then began
to live forever
is more like what he'd say.

Can't you hear him?
                I didn't
pass away but only slipped around

behind you. I'm in the gap
between your words and hiding out,
the way I always was. I did, however,
pass before your eyes once or twice,
back and forth
like reading left to right.
But I don't think you saw me.
I saw you not looking.

My voice passed into language
but is still there, not gone away.
You've got to get your phrases right.
Things depend on it. For example, your life.
The wrong word and you're dead,
or worse, passed away.

I'm William Stafford and I died
in 1993 and will never die again.
My language froze as I got cold.
You can warm it up
if you don't pass away.
Die into my poems instead.
Lie down in them and don't breathe
a word of our secret. Together,
passing from line to line,
you and I will never be dead.

Melody Davis

It Only Starts

The American road is our art,
pure the process of leaving.
Driving doesn't end. It only starts

as the radio feeds a secret part
of the brain that's always running
the American road. Our art

has no destination, though it departs,
and the eyes, never full, keep filling.
Driving doesn't end. It only starts

when the land curls under the car,
as though it were another way of seeing–
the American road, our art,

our music, our motion, our
world spinning by on a string.
Driving doesn't end–it only starts

the drug of this country, too near and far,
where place is endless, beginning
on the American road, an art
of driving that doesn't end. It only starts.

R.P. Dickey

I Have a Daydream Tonight

There should be little doubt that while war has been of great historical interest and drama, governments have killed many times more people in cold blood than they have in the heat of battle. As noted in chapter 2, this is especially true of our century. In any case, governments... clearly should come with a warning label: "This power may be a danger to your life and limb."
—Dr. R.J. Rummel, University of Hawaii, *Murder by Government* (1994), Transaction Publishers, New Brunswick (USA) and London (U.K.)

In the candlelight of this long nightmare
Of all-too-universally-approved
Coercion called History, let me share
A daydream of the new millennium

I have with you. I have a daydream
Tonight near the end of a century
Of governmental murderers who teamed
Up and disrespected many more

Than the 169,198,000 choosers
They murdered for disagreeing with them,
Figuring dissidents to be losers.
Enough children will grow up to rebel

Against the *status quo*, nihilism,
The iron fist of all our yesterdays,
Now euphemistically called pragmatism,
And resist with their lives its servants.

Armed with the vision of their reason they will
By the year 2084 throw off

All irrational state power, or choose
To fight on after the last lights go off.

Lynn Domina

In Lonely Exile Here

His face palsied by rage,
the man on the corner beats
his Bible and heralds
the destruction of me and my kind.
Most often, I keep walking and I don't know

if I stop because today
is the first Sunday
of Advent, and I've already begun humming
0 Come, 0 Come, Emmanuel, and I've already committed
myself to this season of hope,
or because, his bare hands
already chapped, his ears
as red as welts,
he looks so cold in his ridiculous
suede jacket, one button missing from the cuff,
another from the front, that I'm tempted
to give him my own coat,
or because this Sunday
he's brought his son.

The boy has lost one of his mittens
but he warms his hand clapping
to his own imagined jig, made cheerfully awkward
by his rubber boots, and to the rhymes
he's learned to help him remember
words forbidden other children:
> *see a fag, make me gag*
> *send a dyke up the pike*

Turning toward the East River, the approaching flurries,
I remember the last Christmas snow fell through the long night,
waking to make snow angels as perfect
as angels, our yard painfully brilliant
as though a falling star had strewn itself,
prodigally, across our lawn, the woman I loved proclaiming
she felt just like a child.

The boy calls once more:
> *have no fear, kill a queer*

the word trailing after me with the determined rhythm
someone would choose pounding a spike into a rail–
> *queer*
> *queer*
> *queer*

until the Son of God appear.

Susan Donnelly

Harpo

That's right. When words don't say it,
stop talking. Become beautiful and strange.
The one of sudden arrivals,
announced by a horn.

A faun, seen between trees.

Pluck your thin music, your eyes,
getting rounder, face changing
like clouds. And when lies
don't work, even silent ones,

get caught silver-handed,
with everything tucked up your sleeve.

William Doreski

Manhattan Valhalla

A few blocks from Greenwich Village
wooden single-family houses
on square lots trimmed with hedges
have replaced the granite warehouses
and cold brick commercial buildings.

With coffee-to-go in paper cups
from the famous Village coffeehouse
where Duke Ellington met Michael
Jackson, we roam the streets in search
of poets who've died and gone

to this odd Manhattan Valhalla.
The houses, stark white, look old,
repainted many times. They weren't here
last time we roamed this neighborhood
for art galleries and deli.

Perhaps Joel Oppenheimer
and e.e. cummings have met at last
in a lace-curtain parlor where
they can swap favorite obscenities
and mull the decline in culture.

Perhaps Dylan Thomas and Paul
Goodman discuss the latest brands
of beer, and which prodigiously
foam to clot one's poems on one's tongue.
We gaze hard but the windows

resist in tempered gray-tones
and the hedges bristle with thorns.
Odd to roam this suburb with
the downtown skyscrapers looming
less than half a mile to the south.

Odd to drink such powerful coffee
without a jazz band raving
in a badly-lit basement
and the weight of the whole city
causing the brick walls to buckle.

Odd to look forward to dwelling
in such a flimsy neighborhood,
the square imaginary rooms
banked with shelves of small-press journals,
fueled with the smell of damp wool jackets,

bitter talk of grants and prizes,
the beer-breath tough as granite,
oppressive as I plaster my face
to the window and mourn the city
for which we all have gladly died.

Thomas Dorsett

Farewell, Abbie Hoffman,

true American, good man and bad boy;
half in the Jewish prophetic tradition
whose task is to "comfort
      the afflicted and to afflict

the comfortable," you were also
the spoiled, American anti-traditionalist
brat–still loved by Mother in us all:
      "Deep down he's a good boy," we'd say,

"no matter how bad he behaves." Enraged,
a madman, for instance, feeling oppressed
at a match, might blow the stadium up;
      you, just as angry, yet American

as baseball, might thumb your nose at
the umpire, bomb him with explosive words,
yet we'd live, he'd throw you out, and
      both sides would get on with the game.

I remember the time you entered
the courtroom wearing the same
flowing robe as the judge. When he moved
      you moved; we saw our mad world

mocked, as in a childhood circus mirror,
yet with a grown-up message: the judge
was no longer god but flesh, like us,
      Brecht's undressed pope on the stage.

Was your defiance inspired by Marx?
If so, was it Harpo or Karl? Both, Abbie;
you made us see and laugh and strive and
      change; thanks, yahoo saint, and good-bye.

Peter Kane Dufault

DNA

It is unnerving, this
new and apparently
proven hypothesis
of another reality–be-

neath ours, ours where the dead
are, to the living, just
poor uninhabited
silhouettes in the dust–

another reality   down
deeper, down to that very
dust, where a braid or bone–
say, in a reliquary–

possesses the template
of the saint's self   and could,
so we're told, replicate
the original flesh and blood.

It chills mine–the more so
that the high priests of Isis
embalming their Pharaoh
anticipated this.

W.D. Ehrhart

Guns

Again we pass that field
green artillery piece squatting
by the Legion Post on Chelten Avenue,
its ugly little pointed snout
ranged against my daughter's school.

"Did you ever use a gun
like that?" my daughter asks,
and I say, "No, but others did.
I used a smaller gun. A rifle."
She knows I've been to war.

'That's dumb," she says,
and I say, "Yes," and nod
because it was, and nod again
because she doesn't know.
How do you tell a four-year-old

what steel can do to flesh?
How vivid do you dare to get?
How explain a world where men
kill other men deliberately
and call it love of country?

Just eighteen, I killed
a ten-year-old. I didn't know.
He spins across the marketplace
all shattered chest, all eyes and arms.
Do I tell her that? Not yet,

though one day I will have
no choice except to tell her
or to send her into the world
wide-eyed and ignorant.
The boy spins across the years

till he lands in a heap
in another war in another place
where yet another generation
is rudely about to discover
what their fathers never told them.

Susan Eisenberg

Tell Me
for Karen Pollak

What
shall I
do
with the
woman's
hand
left
on the table
of the radial

arm
saw
she was not
instructed
how to use.

It has been
knocking
at the window
of my dreams
poking
in the closet
of my memory
resting
on my shoulder
when I
come home.

What
shall I
do
with that hand
seized
by her
co-workers
and shaken
like an amulet
to exorcise
women
from their midst?

It has been
tearing down
curtains
ringing
bells
writing me
notes
wearing
my rings.

Jim Elledge

606 E. Front St., Bloomington, IL 61701

Staring out this kitchen window at nothing
important, I realize
they were right, those ancient ones whose fingers,
quelling darkness, painted
cavern walls then chipped flint and drank
what blood they

drew; whose raveled tongues became scratches in dust,
song in hardened
clay, litany in marble; whose ears foraged for notes
leaf and wing
gave birth to: sharps, flats, *de-dum de-dum de-dum;*
whose eyes measured,

cubit by cubit, what distance lay between shoe
soles and heaven
then stacked the hell out of the sky until brick after brick
came tumbling down;
whose crimped brows crossed the Alps elephant-back,
shivering at summit.

Somewhere another star
explodes unseen by anyone until after the next
century limps back
to its pen, scarred, exhausted. Somewhere another

layer of silt
feathers, sifting through the current then, at rest,
locks an entire
continent between history's gorgeous teeth.

Somewhere another girl-
child is born to grief to cure the world of itself.
But here, oak
branches crisscross the kitchen window's 3-by-

5 sky busy
as street maps, and a blue jay stops at mid-song,
stares back too
hard, flies off, as a question rises in my throat: Who
needs gravity, anyway?

Jeanne Emmons

Oil Slick

It surges from us, rhythmic, like a corrupt
pulse, clouding the depths, a greasy stain,
pouring out of a rudely opened vein
and blossoming in the suicidal tub.

It billows out like mad Ophelia's gown,
which for a moment buoyed her up, still singing
her aimless song, then with her fist clinging
to the wilted bunch of flowers, dragged her down.

The surf heaves up and paws and slaps its hands.
It pants like a drunken lover. Afterwards
it pulls back, leaving bruises, bodies of birds,
blackened lumps clotting the inert sand.

A cormorant moves beneath a robe of sludge,
dragging a crude drapery on its wings,
weighed down by heavy robes of gabardine,
like an academic, clergyman, or judge.

And on the water there's a bright chain
of dying fish. They stiffen, soften, and bloat,
while dolphins slide into new black coats
and shine like hearses cruising in the rain.

So all the innocents move in the slow sea,
Bobbing in the currents, load on load,
Hauled outward by the driven undertow,
Heron, turtle, grebe and manatee.

Martín Espada

Thanksgiving

This was the first Thanksgiving with my wife's family,
sitting at the stained pine table in the dining room.
The wood stove coughed during her mother's prayer:
Amen and the gravy boat bobbing over fresh linen.
Her father stared into the mashed potatoes
and saw a white battleship floating in the gravy.
Still staring at the mashed potatoes, he began a soliloquy

about the new Navy missiles fired across miles of ocean,
how they could jump into the smokestack of a battleship.
"Now in Korea," he said, "I was a gunner and the people there
ate kimch'i, and it really stinks." Mother complained that no one
was eating the creamed onions. *"Eat, Daddy."* The creamed onions
look like eyeballs, I thought, and then said, "I wish I had missiles
like that." Daddy laughed a 1950's horror movie mad scientist laugh,
and told me he didn't have a missile, but he had his own cannon.
"Daddy, eat the candied yams," Mother hissed, as if he were
a liquored CIA spy telling secrets about military hardware
to some Puerto Rican janitor he met in a bar. "I'm a toolmaker.
I made the cannon myself," he announced, and left the table.
"Daddy's family has been here in the Connecticut Valley since 1680,"
Mother said. "There were Indians here once, but they left."
When I started dating her daughter, Mother called me a half-Black,
but now she spooned candied yams on my plate. I nibbled
at the candied yams. I remembered my own Thanksgivings
in the Bronx, turkey with arroz y habichuelas and plátanos,
and countless cousins swaying to bugalú on the record player
or roaring at my grandmother's Spanish punchlines in the kitchen,
the glowing of her cigarette like a firefly lost in the city. For years
I thought everyone ate rice and beans with turkey at Thanksgiving.
Daddy returned to the table with a cannon, steering the black
iron barrel. "Does that cannon go boom?" I asked. "I fire it
in the backyard at the tombstones," he said. "That cemetery bought
up all our farmland during the Depression. Now we only have
the house." He stared and said nothing, then glanced up suddenly,
like a ghost had tickled his ear. "Want to see me fire it?" he grinned.
"Daddy, fire the cannon after dessert," Mother said. "If I fire
the cannon, I have to take out the cannonballs first," he told me.
He tilted the cannon downward, and cannonballs dropped
from the barrel, thudding on the floor and rolling across
the brown braided rug. Grandmother praised the turkey's thighs,
said she would bring leftovers home to feed her Congo Gray parrot.
I walked with Daddy to the backyard, past the bullet holes
in the door and his pickup truck with the Confederate license plate.
He swiveled the cannon around to face the tombstones
on the other side of the backyard fence. "This way, if I hit anybody,
they're already dead," he declared. He stuffed half a charge
of gunpowder into the cannon, and lit the fuse. From the dining room,
Mother yelled, *"Daddy, no!"* Then the battlefield rumbled

under my feet. My head thundered. Smoke drifted over
the tombstones. Daddy laughed. And I thought: When the first
drunken Pilgrim dragged out the cannon at the first Thanksgiving–
that's when the Indians left.

Rhina P. Espaillat

Bra

What a good fit! But the label says Honduras:
Alas, I am Union forever, yes, both breasts
and the heart between them committed to U.S. labor.

But such a splendid fit! And the label tells me
the woman who made it, bronze as the breasts now in it,
speaks the language I dream in; I count in Spanish

the pesos she made stitching this breast-divider:
will they go for her son's tuition, her daughter's wedding?
The thought is a lovely fit, but oh, the label!

And oh, those pesos that may be pennies, and hard-earned.
Was it son or daughter who made this, unschooled, unwedded?
How old? Fourteen? Ten? That fear is a tight fit.

If only the heart could be worn like the breast, divided,
nosing in two directions for news of the wide world,
sniffing here and there for justice, for mercy.

How burdened every choice is with politics, guilt,
expensive with duty, heavy as breasts in need of
this perfect fit whose label says Honduras.

Pat Falk

On the Beach
Long Island, July 1996

Difficult to focus, to read
the sun sinking westward casts a pall
on water still as glass, and flickering
evening shadows. I look skyward–
geese, gulls, something always passes
by–this time, a plane, exploding.

Children sometimes stare at light
through night-time bedroom windows,
or wide-eyed gaze at lamplight
high on hallway ceilings,
then close their eyes, astonished
at the lingering stark frayed image.

Am I so much the child
that I believe whatever blazes, dazzles,
is so utterly my own–that I deny my own
perception, lose the will to speak?
And what have I seen
except a deeply etched reminder

of the true event–a path of light,
a blast, the shattering of lives,
a shattering distinctly etched
but only a reminder.
I never saw the real thing
but see it now on everything that's real.

Difficult to focus, to feel.
To piece metallic shards into a whole.
To feel beyond a fragmentary fear
that leaves the spirit unredeemed and numb.
The sun sinking westward I look skyward.
Is it dawn, this dome of darkness?
Are those stars or burning stone?

Jim Fairhall

McNamara

I only wanted to be perfect–
not loved, and not all powerful.
I knew my numbers were correct.
I was the one responsible.

I think I was half Prospero,
and half Pythagoras. The end
and the beginning, zero,
I didn't try to comprehend.

But all those digits in between
were airy spirits which, once bid,
uncovered dark things seldom seen:
roots rutting in a sweaty bed,

powers and sexy ratios,
the secret, strange affinities
of numbers stone in love, eros
among the spreadsheets, energies.

Dark energies indeed: but think
of them harnessed by the fierce bright
reins of an Irish Catholic,
a Yank who had fought the good fight

in Europe, who knew that goodness
without bombs and shells and bullets,
and numbers and intelligence,
is as good as a Sunday-school miss–

no power; no tricks; no sex.
I thought that we could win, at first,
even without my *Star Wars* fence.
Wrong, I told the President the worst.

The numbers had *their* way, not mine;
the body count that hurt was ours.
In public still the boss's man,
I held my tongue for thirty years.

And now? All figures are reshaped
by age. Three warrior-kings are gone.
These days–my wizard's rod long snapped–
an old dark prince, my shins unshriven–

I demonstrate (though doubt it's done)
to faces lit on a black wall,
the play of stars and bright-dark men:
not measurable   nor moral.

Charles Fishman

Natural Selection

A new type of giant sponge, previously unknown to science, is growing on thousands of shattered barrels of radioactive waste dumped into the Pacific Ocean....

I wanted a new vase to frame summer's flowers
but nothing ceramic would do, nothing merely
smooth, mauve, streaked, hand-worked. I wanted
something that would hold the twilight without
spilling, would keep the branches and night-
laced leaves and twigs from floating, deserting
the blue nest of the moment. Moonlight held back,
sunlight lingered in the future, and time drifted
in a drugged haze, but nothing could be found
to embrace me. It was the embrace I wanted:
to be sheathed, calmed by approaching darkness,
quieted, fixed in beauty and silence. I knew myself
empty, but your fingers on my face began to heal
me, your soft-lipped words so like the petals
of flowers I could put stems to them. I wanted
a bouquet of nouns and verbs to fill me, a garden
of adjectives. I would cling to shattered barrels,
sway in the current off the Farallon Islands, a new
species: remote, unrepentant, mysterious, blossoming.

Doug Flaherty

Default Mode

I sometimes dream of being a lifeguard at a car wash,
become a midget and pull pimento through olives.
I wish to assume a dramatic presence, be shape-shifted
into a centipede with a lot more shoes to drop.
This country leaves me a bag of neurotic twitches.
My father always said I was a half-bubble off plumb,
but I told him he was comparing kiwi to kumquats.
He laughed, executed a one-handed hand-stand,
intoned that sexual intimations turned him spermicidal.
I told him Shell oil advertises that all you do is
"Pay, pump, and go," making them the first
fossil-fuel bordello in town. In the event you discover
incidental humor, please stop rejoicing.

I turn skitterish in the rush to judgment–
how can we live, knowing the best thing we
can do before the dawn's early glare is to hurry
our own death to stop calamity. The situation:
World War II, three French resistors scuffled over
a dropped cyanide pill as the gestapo rounded them
up for torture. If only there had been a time-machine,
we could have saved them. Where was your time-machine
that bloody Sunday in Birmingham? I lost my map
to Jonestown. More recently, my computer froze-up
on a lesbian-robot video game and wouldn't default.
I was twelve minutes late getting to Oklahoma City.
Yet, in spite of timewarp, reconfigured events, scant
chance to-save-the-now, we know which is mightier:
the word is all we will be left with, if we live.
The sword will kill and bleed us an easy exit.
The whole world might be a stage, but most of us
have forgotten our lines. Hit with the right words, we
can be kept around to be hit again and again. Consider
Descartes–I think, therefore I am. And Sartre–
I am what I do. And Sinatra–Shooby, dooby, do.
Is this a great time to be alive, or what? My father
laughs and undoes his hand-stand. Too much blood
in one spot for too long can make a man think.

Deborah Fleming

Strip Mines

Wine-hearted solitude, our mother the wilderness, men's failures are often as beautiful as men's
    triumphs, but your returnings
Are even more precious than your first presence.
                  –Robinson Jeffers, "Bixby's Landing"

My cousins and I climbed
ridge after ridge of poverty grass and broom sedge,
collected blooms of staghorn sumac,
discovered an orange pool,
found its bottom with limbs of dead trees.

We galloped ponies on trails,
jumped over ditches big shovels had gouged.

I watched clouds bundle up from the west.
The setting sun emblazoned stones

and the Dipper stood on its handle,
enormous in March.

No one—not Hanna Coal nor farmers who sold their land—
cared what you did on abandoned ground.

Now, mining companies have to restore soil.
Hillsides take fifty years to grow back into forest.
Slag heaps never will.

That smooth slope dotted with sheep
was a rugged hill shoved up by glaciers
in the second dawn of its life
and covered by dark woods.

Nothing mined to its core can be reclaimed.

But the strips were good places to ride.
Healing limestone brought back wild cherry and bigtooth aspen.
We galloped in pursuit when deer leaped from high grass
and bounded away, flashing their white tails
like flames.

Stewart Florsheim

Recent Findings

The ingots of gold, they say,
were once the fillings of Jews' teeth
and now the bars are in vaults in Zurich
and New York, in the Federal Reserve Bank,
in fact, where my mother went to work as a statistician
and her bosses calculated the Swiss debt
against the gold that might have belonged
to her aunts or uncles,
the gold they used to chew their boiled beef and potatoes
during family gatherings on Sunday afternoons
where the topic of conversation would be
how quickly all of this madness will pass.

Peter Fogo

Eating Monkeys

The documentary speculated on the origin of AIDS, taking us into remote regions of Angola and Zaire where locals often supplement their normal diets by eating monkeys shot out of trees. Who, although looking somewhat human, were different–qualifying them as food sources during floods and droughts. But as years passed the pressures of deforestation and economic upheaval forced entire populations onto the fringes of unfamiliar forests, where in the shadows of twilight they again shot monkeys who were still, to be sure, different–but now in ways unlike the simians of the old neighborhood.

After that things happened quickly. People fell ill, lost weight, died in agony and disbelief. One promiscuous airline steward took over a thousand trans-Atlantic lovers, inciting plague that ran unabated through gay populations in Europe and North America. Meanwhile, back in Africa, viruses multiplied exponentially as television tolled the death knell in percentages of fatal exposure: Zaire, one in 22; Uganda, one in 17; Zambia, one in 14.

Then silence. White credits rolling on a backdrop of black, punctuated by the network news. Cities held siege in the Balkans. Children gunned down in the streets of Sao Paulo. Sri Lanka, East Timor, Soweto in flames. Sports. Weather. Dow Jones averages and lottery numbers. 10:30 and time enough to haunt bars and coffee houses before last call. Time enough to forget the foolishness of monkey eating and unprotected sex. Time enough to grope for the irresistible comforts of dark intimacy before falling into exhausted slumber, replenishing our spent flesh for survival in the market-driven village where we devour those who are different.

Brett Foster

Armistice to Music

After an October 1995 National Public Radio broadcast in which citizens of Sarajevo reacted to the return of electricity. Many expressed joy at the resumption of American television and pop music.

The orders tolling like an angelus:
Homeless crowd the roads, congest one bus.
Among alfalfa, peacekeepers produce
grave mound-tallies. Life happened, fortuitous.

Diplomats with cognac toast to forego
the gross anatomy of belfries, shame-
faced, gutted, spire bell melted months ago.
So like a church, marked by what is human.

Sarajevo still exists. Wounds, sutures,
its amputations glisten desperately.
Disfigured ironworks of infrastructure.
Medieval buildings kneel like penitents.

Still, garrisons of starlings wing their careless
signatures, dizzy in the afternoon.
Beyond the Balkan chain, imprisoned
roads open, morning-glory's largess–

Gorazde is freed: abrupt, fantastic.
An engineer's wrist turns and natural gas
resurrects the silent city's dim face.

Venice-bound, I hear reports of cease-fire
across the Adriatic. Heavy is a body

of water, and its distance. Now, consider
a different physics, whereby history

in the end is music, gradual, silent
only when it's lived through. All melody

blends disaster and redemption: legato,
measureless. Cafes with their polyphony

of voices rising, enclaves of autumn
violins arranging their sunsets. Light

comes to destitute cities. The solemn
war-torn suburbs calm the military blights.

Imagine Sniper's Alley, water-absent
charnel houses, pylons lined with land-

mines cinching energy once meant to heat
January's snowblown cities, cold as lead.

Catalogue of hardships. One must wonder,
then, at the will to suffer, persevere,

possibly to live, leave a room, render
all the joys and horrors in reverse.

Housework-drunk, survivors vacuum. Just that.
And candle-lit dinners? Memoirs of raids.

But TV stars and Michael Jackson act
as Vesta's peace treaties, the heart's first-aid.

0 give them the music, give them the moonwalk–
They need the magic man, the dancing pants.

Oh pretty young thing! how I want you back–
drifts toward the hills, *oh! give me one more chance*

spills from a shell-shocked high-rise, and bleats
soulfully above a convalescent street.

Linda Nemec Foster

Sitting in America at the End of the Century

I am stuck in a typical 5 o'clock traffic jam
in a nondescript city in the nation's great
mid-section near the end of the hyperbolic,
twentieth century. The car's cassette player
holds a tape from Berlitz–the fast-action
language people–and from the speakers,
wafting through the air like invisible incense,
comes a thick, guttural commotion of sounds
that first rose from that flat plain
on the other side of the world called Poland.
It's a language my grandparents never forgot,
a language my parents refused to remember
on their way to becoming total Americans.
I am stunned by the foreignness of it and
I don't mean just foreign–but alien–not

an immigration agency term–but alien–
as in Venus, Mars, something otherworldly,
not of this planet. At least, my side of it.

This language amuses and frightens me:
like the automated laughing lady
distorted by mirrors in the fun house.
The blurred image of a face I can't quite
recognize–vertigo of awkward boundary and color.

I try to repeat the innocuous phrasing...

What is that?	*Co to jest, tam dalej?*
Do you have milk?	*Czy mozna tu dostac mleko?*
I am lost.	*Zabladzilem.*
Thank you, Mrs. Falska.	*Dziekuje, pani Falska.*

All the while remembering my grandparents,
Marya and Tomasz/Zofia and Franciszek,
at the other end of the century–the wild,
promising beginning of it. They all left Poland
at the same time, mere strangers in a sea
of strangers. No English dictionary, no easy-
to-play cassette tape. Just one suitcase
and eighteen dollars in their collective pockets.
Moving headlong into another century,
another country, and not once looking back.

How could they know that nine decades later
the century would come to its finale like this.
A distant granddaughter surrounded by cars,
afraid of a language that's more akin to damp
earth than linguistics, stuttering in a tongue
so natural to them they know what she's trying
to say, even before the halting words
leave her lips. *Bardzo mi przykro,
nie wiem.* I am sorry. I know nothing.

Philip Fried

Catechism

Does God exist?
                Yes, in a crease,
a crevice, a small room among boulders,
a crack in a wall or a crack in a teacup.
He is here everywhere in our ruin,
pleached and implicated, entangled.

How is He manifest?

                As a piecemeal
pyramid of crumbs carried
by squads of soldier-ants, the noble
helots, centurions, GI Joes,
each crumb of the sublimest sweetness
and together an imminent monument
to creaturely delight.

                And where
shall we worship?
                In the park of darkness
where lamps are set at intervals,
by a riverside at twilight, the boundary
time, the time of illusion, of transit,
of stumbling and love, as the mind's finger-
tips play over the body's zither,
or anywhere that is impure,
that is in and out, like breathing, half-
caste, mystical and gross as breath.

Richard Frost

What I Did in the War

The searchlights crossed in the sky above my lawn,
and my District Warden father and the doc next door
patrolled the walk and kept the blackout safe.
My mother the Block Matron stayed near the phone,
and I the messenger stood by my bike.
A cop car crept along our darkened street.
And nothing happened. All the kits for burns,

the gas masks and the buckets full of sand
grew quaint. There were no bombers good enough
to reach our coast. I hissed the yellow Japs
at the matinee and bought War Savings Stamps.
I saluted and sang and ate the rationed meat.
Then the news got good. One August day
we had a big parade. And that was that.

My father said, "You're in between the wars."
But one came quick, all turned around. We fought
the Chinese while our friends the Japs kept score
and made us cameras and gave us girls
whose eyes their surgeons changed to look like ours.
And then our biggest general got cashiered.
The first three dead Americans I saw
were shot by accident. We watched a hill
and watched it watching us. The enemy
was anyone behind us who said, "Shoot."
And when the bodies festered in the mud,
no one scrambled out to drag them in.
We played with our grenades, we got so bored,
and then came home although we didn't win.

I should have known the next one would be worse.
I watched it every night on my T.V.
in living color. Here a gut-shot cow
lay kicking by a ditch blocked up with kids
and grannies bloating while a pair of hens
ran in circles pecking at the dust.
"It's no big deal," a young lieutenant said.
I watched us spray the jungle and get hooked
in our berets. Meanwhile a mob of boys
in pony tails kept beating at my door
to raise my consciousness. In undershirt
I told them off, brandishing a beer.
I told them I was not the cause of war.
"Go somewhere else," I said. "Give me some peace."

I voted for losers and tidied up my house
and next, a winner started up a war
to give a town back to a company
and won it every day, while some of our
newscasters beamed us pictures of our bombs

threading a green sky. And then our tanks
bulldozed at least a hundred thousand men
into their trenches after stunning them,
a method folks around me were all for.
This rousing month I didn't do a thing
but stand my silent ground. All our guys
and women, but a few, were ferried home
to cheers to make up for the time before
and dignify our will to fight again.

Alice Fulton

About Face

Because life's too short to blush,
I keep my blood tucked in.
I won't be mortified
by what I drive or the flaccid
vivacity of my last dinner party.
I take my cue from statues posing only
in their shoulder pads of snow: all January
you can see them working on their granite tans.

That I woke at an ungainly hour,
stripped of the merchandise that clothed me,
distilled to pure suchness,
means not enough to anyone for me
to confess. I do not suffer
from the excess of taste
that spells embarrassment:
mothers who find their kids unseemly
in their condom earrings,
girls cringing to think
they could be frumpish as their mothers.
Though the late nonerotic Elvis
in his studded gut of jumpsuit
made everybody squeamish, I admit.
Rule one: the King must not elicit pity.

Was the audience afraid of being tainted
–this might rub off on me–
or were they–surrendering–
what a femme word–feeling

solicitous–glimpsing their fragility
in his reversible purples
and unwholesome goldish chains?

At least embarrassment is not an imitation.
It's intimacy for beginners,
the orgasm no one cares to fake.
I almost admire it. I almost wrote despise.

A Little Heart to Heart with the Horizon

Go figure–it's a knitting performance every day,
keeping body and clouds together,
the sky grounded. Simulcast, ecumenical
as everywhere, stay and hedge
against the bet of bouffant space,
you're the binding
commitment so worlds won't split.

Last week we had Thanksgiving.
The post-cold warriors held a summit
full of East meets West
high hopes. Why not hold a horizon?
Something on the level, equitable instead.
They said the U.S. Army held rehearsals
on monastic sand. In the desert,
lieutenants zipped in camouflage
thought back to where horizons were
an unmade bed, a nap
on the world's edge.
Privates, nights
when they were sanded
by flower fitted sheets, ground out
in flower fitted skin: her, oh him.

This Michigan is short on mountains,
long on derricks
needlenosing heaven, making evil
electromagnetic fields.
"Talks on the fringes of
the summit could eclipse
the summit itself," the anchor
admitted. Go figure.

Your reticence, your serene
lowness, because of you I have something
in common with something.
Your beauty is *do unto me* and who am I
to put you in the active voice?
I rest my case
in your repose, a balance
beam, point
blank closure
that won't–bows are too ceremonious–

close. You graduate
in lilac noise. You take off
and you last.
You draw all conclusions
and–erasure, auroral–you
come back. But I am here to vanish
after messing up the emptiness.
I am here to stand
for thanks: how it is
given, hope: how it is
raised. I am here to figure
long division–love–
how it is made.

Cynthia Gallaher

Gulf Sheep

The herds mill about
because they have no pasture,
even the flocks of sheep are desolate.
                              Joel 1:18

To protect us from mines,
the shepherd walks ahead
instead of trailing behind
to round up the usual stragglers,
but what tent could he pitch tonight
to cover us from the black rain?

Who could count hours
     the foul wet tongues
        wagged their fury on our coats,
not even our master who judges

days by the sun's passing,
the sun, blocked and impenetrable
as our smeared and crusted wool.

We, ancient clouds absorbing modem mistakes,
Q-tips in a misbegotten ear,
cotton balls dabbing at a prehistoric oil pan,
Paleolithic intentions would have kept underground,
even a dinosaur's rampage
would only have taken
a few of us at a time.

And though we almost slid
into oil lakes six feet deep,
and saw birds fall out of the sky,
we still could smell the earth
    beyond this desert,
    and green grass
    of the hills where we feed,
somehow, in our hunger, memory,
    or faith in the shepherd
    willing to shatter bone
    for our thick, knotty hides,
we still believed in green.

And alongside the goats, we ate deeply,
    on green hills slicked with sadness,
till the taintedness took our breaths away,
and extinguished us like fire

César A. González-T.

Tocayo[1]
for César Chávez

Tocayo, te fuiste, you left to us
a challenge
great as truth and the beauty of being
one.

---

[1]Tocayo: Namesake; people who have the same given name call one another tocayo, tocaya.

Your colors are the blood-red of dawn, the black of night
of the morning star, the evening star,
of alpha and omega, birth and death
the Tolteca colors of wisdom,
the black and red of Quetzalcóatl *huelguista*
against the entropy of the spirit,
creator of the enigma of people.

You taught us the faith of our fathers and mothers:
que no hay que desesperar
that human darkness must not overwhelm us;
que hay que luchar, that the struggle goes on.
You gave us their will to endure.

Pilipinos, Anglosajónes, Afro-Americanos,
Jews, Protestants, and Catholics,
the great and the least of this world,
the tainted, the tinted, the different and the indifferent,
todos, we all walked with you, César,
who gave joy to our youth.

Fly now, César-Quétzal, son and father of farm workers.
You too are entitled:
Quetzalcóatl, Buddha, Mahatma, Emmanuel;
Christ was your courage, your faith.
As Ghandi and King, you too
called on the divine light within your enemies:
the Son of God in the skinhead
the Divine Child in the bigot
Truth in the posturing politician.

Your great *huelga* was against the silence, the void within.
That was your great reveille for radicals,
what we have received, which we now pass on.

Darcy Gottlieb

This Difficult and Beautiful Life
(in a letter from Delmore Schwartz to R.P. Blackmur)

These have been difficult times
in the century about to end. Hard truths
stare us down. What is irrevocably
lost haunts us between acts of living

as we struggle through darkness
toward new beginnings.

What does it take to begin again
when we are condemned to incompleteness?
When the thorn lives on after the rose
is gone? How do we apologize to the woman
with the swastika carved into her breast?
to the naked and charred corpses tossed
into mass graves–some breathing still
able to feel the shame of their dying–
when innocence is not enough? And guilt
pierces the troubled heart?

If we have known beauty in this life–
and we have–she is the last Goddess
to walk the earth. She comes
in myriad forms when least expected
on ordinary days bringing light
to our being. She makes herself known
in things unseen and meets us face to face
in solitude. She is our Muse
and ultimate love. Because of her
we sing praisesongs of joy and renewal.

Years from now when the future drinks
from the past, O then remember
how the difficult and the beautiful
lay together
in the uneasy bed of our lives.

Matthew Graham

Cold War

I. *Liberty, New York, 1963*
The Weiss boys annexed new territory
In the neighborhood that winter.
We couldn't eat snow because of the testing.
Then missiles locked on Miami and a Mercury space capsule
Sank at sea. And that summer I had to live with my grandmother,
I watched a lattice of sunlight
Slide along the porch.

When I returned the Weiss boys had moved
And an empty peace settled on the neighborhood.
And then somebody shot the president.

II. *Karl Marx Platz, Berlin, 1991*
After stalling for time we departed
At a station whose time had come.
Its tile cornices were still swirled
With the ash of a park burned for fuel.
And time watched from tired windows–
Rearranged by shrapnel and rain–
The distant boulevards widen with light.
Time bought time
Beneath blind surveillance cameras,
And in time whole districts would surrender.
And later, back on the street, with my watch
Stolen or lost, I begged pardon
For the time.

Alvin Greenberg

"me and my shadow"

ted lewis's song as he high-stepped around
the night club stage in a single hot white spot,
top-hatted, tuxedoed, twirling a matching black
cane, his voice whiskey, the words water:

"me . . . and . . . my . . . sha . . . dow"

waiters out here easing their way among white
tablecloths, sliding around the treacherous
edges, the low chatter of diners and drinkers

"strolling down the . . . av . . . e . . . nue"

then another spotlight like a summons in a white
robe, like a whip, like a chain, like a noose
jerking the young black dancer out of the dark,
top-hatted, tuxedoed, his black cane leveled,
slender, handsome, smiling, setting each black
shoe softly down in one of lewis's own footsteps:

"me . . . and . . . my . . . sha . . . dow"

lewis with his silent shadow strolling step
for step behind him down that spotlit avenue,
the waiters for a moment stilled, the diners
glancing up from shadowy plates and glasses...

*

this-is not a scene from some circle of hell.
this is beverly hills country club, ft. thomas,
kentucky, just across the river from cincinnati,
1946, 1948, open gambling in the big back room,

even as a kid i could stroll the plush avenues
of roulette wheels and black jack tables, listen
to the clatter of chips, the croupiers' calls.
and nobody kicked me out. nobody noticed me.

i was a shadow. a shadowy chain linked me
to the table where my parents sat. i didn't know
what they were doing there. i didn't know
what i was doing there. i lived in the shadows.

i talked to shadows. i walked the shadow line.

*

each year a different dancer–younger, slimmer,
sharper–displayed his own quick feet and brief
invention in the one unsung moment lewis stood

aside to give him, leading our applause, then
roping him soon in again with a quick, black
swirl of cane, a tip of the topper, soft shoeing

"me . . . and . . . my . . . sha . . . dow"

leading his boy back down that old dark avenue
while our heads bent again to our muddy plates,
waiters scurrying like fish among our scraps,

the maitre d' my father'd slipped a five to
looking to turn the table for the second show,
and shadows, shadows, even as the lights came up,

shadows every way i turned: shadow of the act
still lingering on the stage above, shadows
at the backroom tables of my mind fingering

shadowy chips and cards, shadows behind, beside
me, and i saw my own shadowy self led off down
some dark avenue without a word, without a dance

to call my own, but not alone: all those sweet
black dancers, ah, six million solemn shadows there
beside me, shuffled away to someone else's song.

William Greenway

Mississippi Moon

Driving home from her father's house
back when we lived down here,
we'd turn the car lights off
and let the full moon silver
the road home. Sometimes we'd even
park and neck.

Back for a visit ten years along,
the skies are busy approaching the millennium.
We go out into the evening to see
the eclipse like a plum with a cap
of sugar, Hale-Bopp chasing
its tail in the solar wind of the southwest,
Orion stalking the skies,
and Mars looking embarrassed
at the jewelry of Venus.

Portents all, prodigies, chimneys tumbling,
and horses eating each other in their stalls,
or at least beavers slapping the water in the dark
and rippling like a TV time warp the stars
and ember eyes of frogs and gators lying on the lake.
Cottonmouths sleep on logs, their mouths
full of moonlight, tired like the snake that swallowed
its tail and made the world, and turtles–like
the one the Natives say the world rests on the back of–
poke their heads from the lake like toes.

No wonder people dream of abduction
by aliens on lonely back roads, city lights
so far way, these stars we thought we knew
moving further from us and from each other.

So when a comet comes calling every
4,000 years or so, we go out and hold hands–
our faces upturned and white as two more moons–
Mars puts blusher over his cracks,
the moon veils her pitted face
and hides her belly with a dark muumuu,
Venus scintillates desperately,
and Orion loosens his belt and holds on,
none of us getting any younger.

Eamon Grennan

Colour Shot

Outside a South African shanty
a line of laundry shines
behind a boy's full, foregrounded face,
his eyes hidden in
enormous orange-rimmed sunglasses.

The washing's a cloud of
white sheets, an umber quilt, three
almond blouses and a fierce
vermillion shirt, all frozen
under a steel and sapphire sky.

The boy stares straight out. A dozen
rusty surfaces come lurching
into splintered light. And behind it all
the rising clear line of fresh washing
gleams in the breeze, a civil sign

and morning offering
to the belief that clean sheets
will mount, like clouds, the air
and swell there, that shirts
will be lathered, rinsed, jounced, wrung out,

then hung to dry and lighten
towards the skin they'll shine on.
In these household flags
of no surrender, these signs
of life that harkens after brightness,

you might find the hearth's
own crooked smoke
ascending, or find
some saving grace to flourish
in the open eye of heaven.

Gordon Grigsby

Shine, Perishing Empire
Homage to Jeffers
"Rise of the West to World Supremacy, 1450–"
Chapter Title, *A World History*

While this "Group of Seven," or Eight, or Fifteen, one-
    fourth of the world's population,
impoverishes the other three-fourths, though they increase,
poisons the Earth, though it begins its revenge,
and settles in the mold of its social violence,
and protest, only a bubble in the molten mass, pops
    and sighs out, and the mass hardens,

I remember ripeness and decadence, out of the mother and
    home to the mother, etcetera,
meteors are not needed less than mountains: shine,
    perishing empire–these jeweled cities
at night, these drums of uranium glowing like Madame Curie's hands
under the seas, these wings of high-tech bombers
flashing to punish some Third World country with three
    thousand strikes a day.

Well, we used to kill Indians and keep slaves.

To become human is to enlarge the mind and invent cruelty.
    It's either ignorance or sorrow,
the old myth says.
        But how to deepen knowledge and live,
with no immortal illusions, outside of history–
that's what the old poet lived to say.

Mac Hammond

The Year 2000

I am almost tempted to give up
Smoking so I might live to see the year 2000.
I imagine on that New Year's Eve that–
The crowd in Times Square ready to explode–
Some religious nut will set off
His homemade atom bomb in New York
And, then, trigger-happy generals all
Over the world will push their buttons
And the earth will be consumed in fire,
A chain reaction so intense that the oceans
Will turn to hydrogen and oxygen gas
And burn. Or I imagine the beginning
Of the third millennium will be followed
By a breath-taking silence so profound
That the room I am in will bleed at the walls
And the fire in the fireplace will be extinguished
By *Lacrima Christi*. Or I imagine the end
Of 2000 years will dawn the same as yesterday
And the earth will wait several billion
Years to be engulfed, at last, by the dying sun.
Anyway, what's left of me, what's left
Of us all, our scattered bodies, pictures,
Poems, will disintegrate, all form gone,
Only some atoms, random and insane,
In some black hole. I say sooner
Or later, so what's the dif, if I take care
Of my health or not, if I stop smoking or not.

Stephen Haven

Near the Millennium

I think of how they came here clinging
to that first shore, a thin
strip of sand, and Mrs. Bradford
over the edge, off the starboard stern
at the first hint of land, how they sold
to come here, most of what they had,

and what they didn't have yet,
promising investors
in that early venture, free
enterprise, a lifelong temporal dance
with spiritual ends
and natural dividends, whatever—
fish, timber, fur—
they could wrestle from the land.

Such innocence! to set out so late,
in September, set up in Plymouth
in December, the 21st to be exact
measuring by our calendar...
Such courage, such foolishness
to think their lives
mattered in God's eyes...
Delayed in Liverpool
by one or another leaky vessel,
they wouldn't turn back, even when
August burned autumn red.

I can hardly imagine it, even now,
in summer, in Provincetown,
Cape Herring Bay, 8:00 A.M.,
June 28th, a Wednesday,
the sea lapping the shore
like a dog its master's hand,
as if, in 1995, in the cross
they bore, their indigenous
distinction between the natural,
the human, there were only
inviolable reciprocity.

But even on such a day, blue blue sky,
blue waves, I can't dream
of landing here, winter distant
or winter near, to search
for a good spring,
safe bay, and land that might
bring corn to the few
who came singing what they knew
or thought they knew of God's name.
Fish for all of England! Cod

for the tired refuge
of Europe's sinful shores!
For Plymouth's children
and for their children's children!
What more came of it than cash or corn

is hard to say. Something remains.
They drift in and out of view.
In school I learned about
their special civic trust,
one man one vote in the first
Massachusetts church (no one told us
the unconverted and women didn't count).

Then, especially on my drive in,
carefully marked on Route 6
so tourists wouldn't miss it
one beach, one commemoration
of our first shots
of race against race
the tone of which wasn't a lament.

The millennium nears
here in P'town as everywhere.
Still, I think of them
in their first season,
how they died like bees
drugged by the way the planet tilts
each fall toward Halloween.

I'll say this much for them:
in all they did they took
the chance to live, as if
the quicksand of their lives
might open to the sky.
Short of this, all else
at risk, here on the same
strip of sand, or near,
they are our cracked seeds,
we are the split ends
of their leafy dividends.

Elegy for Larry Levis

Now one last cigarette
the one he didn't get
and all he has to say is this:

drift, drift.

He was almost young.
One didn't have to know him well
one didn't have to love his poetry to feel
the indigenous weight of it.

A drop of Spanish blood.

Now, if he sings of California,
Lorca's black elf
grins over his left shoulder.

De Soto, floating in his ossuary,
whistles through cracked teeth.

Now his work in the form
of a moth on a dark sill,
moth on the mouth of where
he'd ever been. Or else the poem

of his old age
a mythic vintage
year that will never come.

The quiet of his voice, tonight:

Cognac, cognac on the tongue.

Hunt Hawkins

G-Man

Didn't we always know J. Edgar Hoover
was like that? Of course, by our principle
that something must produce its opposite,
like castles giving way to towns,
the fletchers zinging from courtyard to guildhall.
In the '40s he wore long-hemmed dresses
with shoulder pads, later pedal pushers
and poodle skirts, then pillbox hats, the styles

with which America has tortured its women.
Being a vassal was no picnic.
You gave most of your crop to the lord,
then he dragged you off on a Crusade,
your only weapon a sharpened stick.
To cap it off, he got your bride that first night.
Still, when blood-dripping Huns appeared over the hill,
someone was supposed to take care of you.
In the towns, nobody gave tuppence if the cooper's
apprentice lived or died. Of the two Edgars,
then, which was our friend? Was it the tough guy
who photographed JFK coming out of that
German woman's apartment in the early hours,
wiretapped King in Montgomery, let blackmailing
Lansky loose to cram the ghettoes with drugs,
junkies dying in empty lots with needles
hanging from their arms? In the event
that somebody from the Bureau should be
reading this, please know I'm only kidding.
Poetry makes nothing happen. We lost
our audience ages ago. Still, I like to think
of Edgar stripping down, G-man in G-string,
the closest we'll ever have to a true protector.

The Invisible Hand Meets the Dead Hand
High above Washington, D.C.

There! in the clouds can't you see
the Invisible Hand prancing, tumbling?
It soars over the Reflecting Pool,
pirouettes atop the Washington Monument.
I think it must be Adam Smith's,
the Hand he said would harmonize
all selfish interests, miraculously making whole
a society of pure individuals. Down on the ground
thousands of portly men wearing Adam Smith ties
adore this Hand as they circle the obelisk,
their hair slicked back and their flies open.
Then suddenly they squat, the flesh of their
upper arms quivering, and in unison croak:
"Ketchup is a vegetable! No new taxes!"
I figure them to be fiscal conservatives

because they set out buckets full of loopholes
into which they piss, claiming confirmation
of the trickle-down theory. Next they chant:
"Death to welfare queens! Send in the Marines!"
With arm gestures, they indicate their belief
that government should be small, but the army big
because democracy must be defended even in
caliphates. And what is the Dead Hand doing here,
this skeletal yellow apparition? O, it just came
to party. It chases the Invisible Hand, busy dancing
in the sky like Mickey Mouse's immaculate glove.
They clasp, shake, high five, then start to tango.

George Held

Inauguration (1997) Sestina

Snowflakes soar on the updraft between cars
As my train switches engines, heading south.
From NY to DC we're mostly white;
From DC south we become mainly black,
The capital dividing the nation
As electric yields to diesel power.

It's Inauguration Weekend: the power
To govern rests with Clinton despite cares
That some scandal will unseat the nation's
Leader, send him slinking home to the South
Impeached, his reputation so blackened
That even Newt's by comparison looks white.

Our national soap opera: Can white
Men dominate the blackened halls of power
Much longer? Can whites oversee blacks
Of the generation seated in this car–
Savvy, sanguine, and cool restored down South,
Ready to emancipate the nation,

Grant absolution for the damnation
Of racism? All these abstractions whitewash
The suppurating gash of hate, Southern
Born but long nurtured in dreams of white power
Up North: ship all the Others in boxcars

To a new Dachau, a final blackout.

Had Lincoln lived, clothed in typical black
He'd have presided over our nation
A hundred years ago, worn by the cares
Of Reconstruction. Clinton, plagued by White
Water, has no great cause and no great power
As we face four more years of going south.

I go to the capital of the South,
Where Monument Ave. honors its first black
And Lee / Jackson / King Day nods to the power
Of blacks, where fear of miscegenation,
Like cancer, still haunts the rebellious whites
Who display the Stars and Bars on their cars.

Like sand in dunes power shifts in the South
And in this nation: together might black
And white overcome internecine cares?

Michael Heller

To Postmodernity

Some of the poets have discovered
that we are anxious to disconnect
the dots and words, to invoke
speech's possible ramble
coming in, awash and surrounding
like a tide, like a tide
of dead leaves whispering
our autumnal contingencies.

And true, the clichés abound,
exposing our non-being
and the certain emptiness of death,
the passivity needed to survive
the modern by luxuriant asides.

And yet love's obliquity
is still a language,
a tutoring mastery of desires
and hurts, leaps and kneelings
at the utterance of a name.

Robert Hershon

Light and Dark, East and West
For Sherman Alexie

Out west there is apparently such a dearth of
African Americans that they must use Native Americans
as niggers, so during his first visit to Brooklyn,
when Sherman went to the store with Donna,
he was amazed that the manager didn't watch him
from the end of every aisle to ensure that he wasn't
boosting cupcakes, "and me with a white woman, too"
except the manager is Lebanese and it's business as usual.
On the subway I point out other models:
If you lived here, you could be Pakistani one day
Puerto Rican the next and Algerian on Sundays.

      Why do you think of yourself as so dark, you don't
look so dark to me, says Larry, whose nephew is
Jewish-Italian-Korean, whose former wife is Japanese-
Czechoslovakian. Where I live, Sherman tells him,
you'd be dark.

      And zoom here I am in America talking to
Americans. Guy on an outlet mall bench in Utah, in NRA cap,
says he's never been in New York but "I'm an American.
I'll walk anywhere I like." I'd like to drop him off in
Red Hook one night, where you don't hear many cowboy tunes.

The westerners all talk about being westerners
and what it means to be a westerner and what do
people in the east really think about Wyoming
(actually, nothing) and they are open and friendly
so if I say I'm talking to "a perfectly pleasant man"
it's foreshadowing of plot and I am indeed talking
to such a man, about how Mormons have large families,
about how every small religion finds theological reasons
to have a dozen children. Very similar
to the Chassidim in New York, I note. Except, he says,
the Mormons don't have a lot of money.

In Vancouver's Chinatown we can't find an open restaurant
but every doorway has a black hooker and an Indian wino
so why isn't it called Hooker Town, Wino Town,
Dead-Eyed-And-Washed-Up Town, Let-Down Fall-Down

Break-Down Town, Curse-God-And-Die Town,
End-Of-The-Line-For-You-Babe Town, so we walk on to
Gastown, which used to be skid row, but is now scrubbed
and open for business–jazz bars, burden baskets
and veal scaloppine.

On the Washington coast, everyone has a personal sunset over the bay
and asks hey, when are you going to move here?
and there are espresso booths at the powwow
What, you've never seen grass dancers at the powwow?
What, you've never seen mad Lubavichers dancing
down the middle of Eastern Parkway?
Even now, Haitian cab drivers who cannot get across
are snarling at their Russian passengers
but the drivers from Calcutta have already started to roll
for who is more dangerous and carefree than a New York cab driver
with a guarantee of paradise.

Donna Hilbert

Vanguard Barbie Gets Fitted

It was no consolation to Barbie that Bill had been fitted a few days earlier; he was, after all, several years older and although quite sexy, certainly no symbol. It's true they're as tiny and pink as her nipples would be, were she allowed to have them. And her lustrous hair could easily be styled to cover them, but she would know they were there and that made her feel an eensy bit deceitful–used as she was to having her plastic protuberances up-front where she and everyone else could admire them.

Barbie wondered how she'd ended up deaf. Perhaps it was the rock concerts she and Ken used to go to, or the years of driving the Vette through Malibu Canyon, stereo cranked up to cover the wind. By the time her second husband, G.I. Joe, was down-sized by the army and could fit easily into all of her vehicles, she was already having trouble in the upper registers, unable to hear sirens or *any* early warning signals.

Joe commandeered her and her camper to use in his new gardening business, insisting she looked sexy with the leaf-blower strapped to her back. Soon her days were filled blowing lawns owned by guys like her ex-husband Ken, who by now she realized was not the only man in the world without balls. And at least he wasn't mean like Joe, who banged her head into the side of the camper–now their permanent home–when she refused to join the militia.

At first it wasn't so bad being deaf to the mower, the blower and Joe. But soon the lack of outside noise caused her to hear some icky thoughts in her head—like how she would always be childless. It didn't seem fair that she had magnificent breasts, but no vagina. Midge said what, with Ken and Joe's obvious deficits, would she *do* with one anyway? But she thought the old saying, "give a boy a hammer and he'll soon find something to pound," might apply in this case.

Her whole life was invested in looking good, being a good companion, playing the game. She hoped things would be different for Skipper. She forced the Barbie pink hearing aids into her ears, her first accessory to penetrate plastic.

Jane Hirshfield

Jasmine

"Almost the twenty-first century"–
how quickly the thought will grow dated,
even quaint.

Our hopes, our future,
will pass like the hopes and futures of others.

And all our anxieties and terrors,
nights of sleeplessness,
griefs,
will appear then as they truly are–

Stumbling, delirious bees in the tea scent of jasmine.

Daniel Hoffman

In the Gallery

Here neither nymph nor naiad ever bathed
nor saint refreshed herself in pristine water,

here, in The Gallery, between Tie Rack,
Camera Shop, B. Dalton, Radio Shack,

Dad's Pizzas, Software, Message Cards, and Chez
Chocolat, a stream and pool's contained

by marble, or simulated marble, banks
with fountains on two levels and a water-

fall, the pumped recycled water's
splash and gurgles cool or seem to cool

the loud bright air so filled with crowds and hawkers,
bottom agleam with shining coins whose shimmer

reflects the neon clash of colors flashing
on pennies aglitter, gleaming quarters, dimes

tossed in from the concrete shores or flung
from the arched bridge that joins one aisle

of bargains to the other, each coin thrown
with a silent, urgent wish to some power unseen–

Dear Goddess of Good Luck, whatever your name now,
please smile on us, who make this place your grove.

Frances Hunter

March 1992
(Johannesburg)

Earth cracks and creaks on a summer's back;
each day breaks, sways, swirls with heat and voices.
Some die beside trains, at funerals, in hostels, on roads,
in beds–they are gone–others simply breathe, bleed,
cry, and go to work, and the maize crop fails
while giants on Olympus meet and talk.

Under the steel-bright sky come tidings–
El Niño, global warming, dangerous holes in the sky–
and the giants talk of interim government, constitution
and referendum and we hear these words while the
dome above swoons its way from break to setting,
thundering without rain in the afternoons, and we ruminate.

Though we have no rain, we also have media thundering
of widespread recession, unemployment, and famine.
While the sky stays bold, far away, and withholding,
most of us keep our heads down, going doggedly on,
but one of us whispers about population explosion and AIDS–
the sky roars–and he wonders if such a thought can kill.

There's a slow dimming of the summer glare, but
the resounding reverberation goes on, with no end to it,

no beginning, no end, no way of fitting it all into
a grain of sand, finding it in an innocent hedgerow,
and nothing auspicious comes down from the giants,
from the sky, from the invisible holes above.

Kathleen Iddings

Maple Rocker

Unpredictable as a March wind, Mother howled
around the farm in her flannel granny-gown
under a cold moon. Sockets of space had
replaced her Valedictorian,
                        Book-of-the-Month mind.

Though she'd strayed back to the long
rope-swing of childhood, Father swore he'd
never *put her away*. Not even when she painted
the kitchen walls with feces
                        as he slept.

But his nerves frayed like the old Philco radio-cord
jerked from the wall too often. A family
conference was called. Nursing-home plans made.
"She'd not even know,"
                        we, her children, reasoned.

Mother's eyes darted from child to child
like a scared hen when a stranger approaches.
As we eased her toward the door, false-teeth and
glasses in a small bag, some half dead synapse
connected in the nether-world of her mind
and she knew
                        she was leaving home forever.

"No!" she screamed grasping the great oak table,
"Don't take me away!" We loosed her hands
from the table where she'd fed nine of us,
and the maple rocker where she'd nursed all of us,
and carried our mother
                        out the back door.

Ruth G. Iodice

Towards Ithaca
for Harold, who loving us, wrote us all in
"Ithaca has given you the beautiful voyage."
　　　　　　–Cavafy, 1911

Not far from the sea's resounding waves a child
hears outside his window the tremolo
of birdsong so sweet he is beguiled–
longs to soar and become that bird–go
out into the night–Later, in mountains,
then in a hidden canyon rimmed with trees–
on a sundrenched deck–he sits and trains
his pen ever through the winedark sea.
Steering through dreaded strait he weaves
betwixt Scylla and Whirlpool–Cyclops and Enchantress–
till storm-tossed and ill in the end
he gives back to the sea that richesse
it gave him–earth, water, fire, air–
arrived at last at Ithaca the fair.

Bonnie Jacobson

Waving to Nemerov

Was that him? did he get off all right? we asked
shielding our eyes against a glint of plane,
the world as usual a beat

late and a hair uncertain about its
poet heroes and their campaigns, but
nevertheless climb he did and dip his wings,

thumbs up in his final finicky flight
of beloved language, still Trying Conclusions,
still getting them right.

Maggie Jaffe

For Lewis B. Puller, Jr.
Our stumps are all tangled up.

Chesty pulled more than his weight.
The Marine Corps had to love him,

couldn't pin enough medals
on his chest for fighting 5
wars & for having a son.
*Dad taught me to stand for ladies
& to shake a man's hand firmly.*

But life rushes right by a man.
In a *flash*–Virginia childhood, to San Diego,
to the triple-canopied jungle–steps on a
booby-trapped howitzer round,
vaporized legs, pink mist surrounds him.
Pray, Lieutenant, for God's sake, pray.
Screams come from another country.
Years later, Pain still walks point for him.

Back in the World
a wife & kids, booze & painkillers.
Demands clemency for vets who've deserted,
then loses a bid for Congress.
A '91 photo shows clench-jawed
Puller in front of the Wall:
his wheelchair mirrored
in the smooth granite surface.

May 11, 1994: Lewis B. Puller, Jr.
died of a *self-inflicted wound*
19 years after the war's end,
the average age of a grunt in Vietnam.

David Jauss

Homage to John Cage
Silence is so accurate.
         –Mark Rothko

Light through vaulted windows, the shadows
of elms in wind. On stage, the pianist,
hands in his lap. Still. The shadows
strumming his face, his hands. Four minutes

and thirty-three seconds of silence
so you may hear the music
of conditioned air through vents,
rustling clothes, the muffling echo

of shoes shuffling, all the sounds
the orchestra of chance performs.
The whole world is an auditorium.
But halfway through, those sounds fade

and you're lost in the labyrinth
of the ear, listening to the sea
of blood drumming the tympanum, the surf
of sound waves spiraling in the cochlea,

the neurons singing synapse. You're inside
the silence so far, your body
is the only world. So it's a shock
when someone coughs and brings you back

to this unreal room, a shadow
watching shadows, an echo
hearing echoes, like the souls
chained in Plato's cave. Your life flickers

on death's wall. What music can transform
shadow to substance, echo
to original score?
Your heart repeats its one note

and you listen harder, a musician now,
as the shadows drift
across the stage like snow
and find you silent, bereft.

Vincent Katz

Ciao, Jim

Looking down at Jim Merrill's obituary,
I have to smile.
I always smile when I think of him.
Death didn't surprise Jim, was something
he prepared for all his life–

poems, deep travel, that Greek sense
of eternity printed in a temple sky:
a young boy's dirty thigh.
His love of opera (and of life)
carried him far above the vagaries

of professional acts, personal deceit;
he decided his lover, life, with lifelong
friend, collaborator David Jackson.
Strange bits of verbiage accosted him
in Hagia Sophia, blowjob on the corner.

He had the charm to ingratiate the great
and humble, Arab, Greek, Italian–
he composed his poems as seer
for an age; early success separated him
from a world; another beckoned.

He trained sights on it, closing eyes.
Maintained contacts, found words perfect-
suited to his non-mission: simply
be Jim. Took his place at the
Greek table. The light

was different, causing other spawns of note,
the furtive faun-thrusts no more a part
of life than simple honey-cake, centuries'
repartee. I have to smile when I see
Jim's spritelike look of pulled

innocence. What remains is not
decisions, awards, but an eager
thrusting of words, athletic dissembling
of advanced copulation. He appeared
capable of receiving divine imprint,

oracle, Pythian priestess, drunk on insight,
his life turned into books
(we should be so lucky), he went
to start health regimen, and died:
The poet in lemon-peel dawn.

X.J. Kennedy

Then and Now

I half-desire those crappy days again
    When babies used to be produced by sex,
Back before women washed their hands of men
    And switched to being corporate execs.

Now, nearing forty, weary of their own
   Private Lear-jets with uniformed wine-tasters,
They tap the sperm bank for a little loan,
   Inseminate themselves with turkey-basters.

Those were the days of pumpkin pie and dads
   Rigging kids kites, grim days of no divorce,
of home-brought bacon, nights out with the lads,
   And mooseheads goggling from the mortgaged walls.
God was no vaguely feminine life-force
   But old Pop Yahweh, hung with beard and balls.

For Allen Ginsberg

Ginsberg, Ginsberg, burning bright,
Taunter of the ultra right,
What blink of the Buddha's eye
Chose the day for you to die?

Queer pied piper, howling wild,
Mantra-minded flower child,
Queen of Maytime, misrule's lord
Bawling, *Drop out! All aboard!*

Finger-cymbaled, chanting *Om*,
Foe of fascist, bane of bomb,
Proper poets' thorn-in-side,
Turner of a whole time's tide,

Who can fill your sloppy shoes?
What a catch for Death. We lose
Glee and sweetness, freaky light,
Ginsberg, Ginsberg, burning bright.

<u>Shirley Kishyama</u>

Notre Dame, 1995

I. On Ile de la Cite, stands Our Lady, not a mother
bountiful, but hallowed vessel chosen by the all-supreme
God. The buttressed cathedral is earthbound, vainly striving
to fly to heaven, inhabit sky, float among the clouds,
shower us with mercy although we've sinned, let us go on
walking as upright men while The Blood of the Innocents

fertilizes the ground. From this same isle innocent
Jews were deported to the death camps while the hollowed mother,
gazed into the setting sun and cast a long shadow on
the boats and trains screaming east, orchestrated in supreme,
precise, industrialized death. On that far horizon, clouds
of human rain stormed and spilt ash as Rene Buscay, striving

to please the Nazis as Chief of Police of Paris, striving
to outdo them all, found two hundred thousand innocents.
Never brought to trial, he flourished after the war. Clouds
of Mitterand's power shrouded him like loveblind mothers
protect terrible infants and let them reign supreme,
godlings with underdeveloped brains and hearts.   II. Upon

our sleeves we do not wear swastikas as we place marks on
the heads of immigrants, lesbians and gays. While striving
to keep taxes low, the kingdom pure, and God's word supreme,
we need not quote LePen or Hitler. We maintain innocence
as we ask the people to turn against father, mother,
sister, brother; chant family values in a culture that clouds

the worth of the one who births, a culture plagued with killing clouds.
It's now fifty years since Normandie. The cycle also turns
on Hiroshima, Nagasaki and Anna Frank, a mother
never pregnant but the parent of hope for those striving
to embrace the simple belief mirrored in her innocent
dark eyes. She believed that people are good. In the supreme

design, if we're to believe we're made in His own supreme
image and that His kind of justice thunders down from the clouds,
where does Anna Frank's death fit? Her sacrificed innocence
rips open heaven like the atomic bombs we dropped on
two cities, vaporizing all we call fair. We're striding
the earth like a father that beats his children and their mother.

And still, Anna Frank's supreme faith circles us like the moon.
We queue beneath sun or clouds, waiting to climb the attic stairs, striving
to resurrect innocence. Let us weep for the virgin mother.

Carolyn Kizer

Fin-de-Siècle Blues

I.
At seventeen I'm told to write a paper
on "My Philosophy": unconscious Emersonian
clone, courtesy of my Father,
"There is no evil," that's what I say,
"merely the absence of good." I read the papers.
Where was my head? (In the clouds, like Father
and the senior William James.) I must have known
some of the bad news. No evil, eh?
Ho, Ho, Ho, Holocaust! Tell it to the Jews.

I wrote another paper, worrying
about the fate of historic monuments,
Art, not people, during World War II.
Give me that tired query from Ethics 101
concerning the old lady and a Rembrandt etching
in a sinking rowboat: which one would I save?
Now that I *am* one, still I have serious doubts
about saving the old lady.
Rembrandt would have won.
And if they could have been crammed into the rowboat
so would the French cathedrals and the Parthenon.
(There was some kind of screaming aesthete
naked within my transparent ethical overcoat.)

But now, take Sarajevo: Old ladies, buildings,
children, art; all perish together
along with honor and philosophy;
the hypothetical rowboat long since sunk
in the polluted Mediterranean sea.
The century suffers entropy–and so do I.

II.
Well, it's been one hell of a century:
Endless lists of victims, Armenians, Jews,
Gypsies, Russians, Vietnamese,
the Bosnians, the Somalians,
torture and rape of the dissidents all over
the map; and as Time winds down

the music slows,
grows scratchier, plays off-key,
America chimes in with its own obbligatos:
what we did to the Nicaraguans, the Salvadorians,
diminuendos with Granadans, Panamanians–
and we're still hassling poor old Castro.

Whole continents go on living under tyrannies
till tyrannies give way
to chaos and criminality.
Is it the horror, or that we know
about the horror–this evening's blood
on the screen?
Yugoslavia, before our eyes, is Balkanized
to death; but today, brave us,
today we recognized Macedonia.
(Vasco is dead, thank God,
and how are you faring, dear Bogomil?)

Then we have AIDS...
Maurice, Tom, Tony, Gordon, Jim, Peter, Bill,
bitterly I mourn you
and wait for the next beloved name.
The red-neck senators who would starve the Arts
are a less efficient scourge.
We who are merely witnesses
to all this grief
also pay a price.
NOT AN ORIGINAL THOUGHT
(that's part of the price).

Horror numbs.
Violence, whether fictional or true,
is socially addictive.
NOT AN ORIGINAL THOUGHT
Serious satire undermined
by sexual and political
grotesquerie.
NOT AN ORIGINAL THOUGHT
So why go on? I'm blue. Boo-hoo.
Got those End-of-the-Century blues.

III.
Now to personalize and trivialize the topic,
as writers, what are we to do?
We gag on scandal, our lives are gossip fodder.
In our marginal way, we are becoming stars.
Never mind the work. Who cares for that?
Did the man who reinvented the sonnet
urinate in his bed one night when drunk?
Did our great fat nature poet
throw up in his hat?
Forget the revolution they created
with their raw confessional poetry;
it's the suicides of two women
which fascinate,
not their way of working
but their way of death.

O you serious men and women
who wrote your poems, met your classes,
counseled your students, kept your friends
and sent magic letters home,
your lives are pillaged and rearranged
by avid biographers who boast that they tell all,
so it seems you always reeled in a mad whirl
of alcohol, abandonment and sexual betrayal.
(I sorrow for the stain on your memory,
Anne, Randall, Ted, Elizabeth,
Delmore, John, and Cal.)

As writers, what are we to do?
Our roles as witnesses ignored,
our fine antennae blunted
by horror piled on horror,
our private matters open
to the scrutiny of voyeurs.
If we have wit and learning
it's met with the apathy
of the ever-more-ignorant young.
How do we hope to carry on
in the last gasp of the millennium?

Much as we always have: writing for one another,
for the friends we tried to impress in school

(like Tonio Krüger), for the dead father or mother,
for our first mentor, compassionate and cool,
for the dead authors who watch over us.
We'll write when bored in strange hotel rooms,
we'll write when the conscience pricks,
we'll write from passion, present or reviving,
making copy of our pains or perverse kicks.
We'll write if a cookie dipped in tea
transports us to the fields of memory.

But first of all we'll do it for ourselves,
selfish and narcissistic and obsessed as ever,
invading the privacy of those who care for us,
spilling sad secrets confided by a lover.
We take note of the café where Valéry took notes,
Van Gogh's yellow chair, the monastery
where Murasaki wrote, as Petrarch did,
in a room eight feet by three;
name-and place-dropping, grooming our fur,
fanning and shaking our peacock tails
(dry sticks rattling in the wind),
always, always ourselves our own mirrors.

The burden of our song: good luck to the young!
Let's drink (for we drink) to a better world
for them, if they should live so long.
As my father the optimist used to say,
"It's the unexpected that happens."
There is little point in being fatalistic;
whatever occurs will be different from
what we anticipate,
which, to be frank, is universal doom.

Everyone who reads this is older than Mozart,
than Masaccio, than Keats, much older than Chatterton.
We're taller, handsomer, healthier than they.
So let's just count these years we've lived as velvet
as Carver said at the end–sweet Ray.
I'm blessed by parents, children, husband, friends
for now... Nothing can take that away.
NOT AN ORIGINAL THOUGHT
Call up Voltaire. Tend the garden.
Seize the day.

Steve Kronen

For L, Born August 6, 1945

A ring floats about your ankles
where the dew has soaked the circle

of your dress: a gray halo that sways
forward with the body displacing

the grass before it. When Newton
considered this world, the atom's

capacity to harbor light
was undreamed of; only its weight

and how it drew one body
to another the way God

would one day draw to his bosom
the scattered flock of his Chosen

as he descended to this planet,
terrible and effulgent.

Since then, science has
perfected its appliances

making the body-electric
almost palpable; atomic

and subatomic, so by 'forty-
five we could prepare a sortie

to glide slowly over Hiro-
shima and above ground-zero

release its burden.
                   On the wall
above our bed you've tacked a small

picture from that day. The photo
of a man, rather the shadow

of a man, who, when caught mid-stride
had his image thrown on the side-

walk before him as on a frame
of unexposed film.

Nothing remains of that man; not flesh
or muscle or bone or ash,

only that blackened silhouette
spread on the walk by the sudden white

flash that made his skeleton
shine for a moment through his skin

before he utterly disappeared.
It has now been forty-four years

since that day and we go on
with our lives as if nothing's wrong.

Tonight that photograph will shine
down on your empty dress like the moon

across a summer lake.
And again that picture will wake

you from your sleep and you'll press
yourself against me as if our flesh

were two halves of a greater whole,
the common vessel for each soul,

as if matter, divided, could bond
itself and heal forever the wound

that separates it.

Marilyn Krysl

Suite for Kokodicholai, Sri Lanka

1. *Daughter*
My mother's name was Mamangam Maheswary
We thought many together would be safe
When you're afraid, a crowd seems good
I believed in the mill I could hide my children

My mother sat down in the center of the room
Her sari was red, the color of heat
The rest of us scurried like rats   She was calm
The soldiers' shouts sounded like shots

I pushed my children back, behind the others

My mother's back the spine of a queen
Like an old tree she had grown strong
I have seen grown men tremble in her presence

But these soldiers were not men, nor am I woman
Like a rat I hid beneath my dead children
My mother sat like a stone carving
Her full name was Mamangam Maheswary

2. *Husband*
I was in my fields when I heard the first shots
I walked quickly   The houses were empty
I could hear the soldiers ahead, firing
Then I met others, also walking quickly

We came to Kumaranayagam's mill
Beside the gate red blossoms of hibiscus
The gate stood open   Beyond I saw my wife
She stood in the compound as though she owned nothing

Inside a strip of light lay across the floor
A woman knelt dipping a cloth in a bucket
Again and again she washed the same stain
The stain began to gleam, as though polished

My wife had laid our children side by side
She had placed the smallest between the other two
She had laid the boy between his two sisters
They liked to walk that way, one on either side

3. *Wife*
After the mine the soldiers came
Among those men they took was my husband
They made the men circle the crater three times
Then the soldiers forced them into the center

The third one herded in was my husband
Where I stood I could see his face as they shot him
I watched as one by one the others fell
Their bodies one above the other, sticks of wood

I have seven children   I know my husband's body
After the burning I did not know his body
After the burning I did not see his face again
This cloth is a piece of his sarong, partly burned

Barbara F. Lefcowitz

Goodbye 20th Century

Like the generous ocean when it combines its blueness with the less emphatic blue of tidal grass, so I offer to hold your thin, leathery hand, ease your dying. You couldn't help all that shed blood: Hitler, Stalin, Mao were not born on your watch and if only you had known the potential of a split atom surely you would have saved Hiroshima.

Remember how proudly you greeted those first mornings' wobbly steps, how you marveled at your early moons, as if none had shone before? Those tightly-strung men and women you inherited: did you not applaud when they spun to a ragtime waltz, slowing untying each cord? You had big plans for them, The Palladium, Covent Garden, the works. Remember when you first heard Mozart from somewhere inside a wooden box, saw a distant face on a screen?

And that boisterous party anticipating your 100th birthday! Compact disks and fax machines sharing microwaved popcorn with a jazz quartet and a jet plane, antibiotics dancing on the World Wide Web, nylon embracing teflon, lasers penetrating polyester hearts; "The Wasteland" so wildly drunk from one plastic cup of vitamin-fortified punch it rolled on the vinyl floor, caroused with a couple of Pound's Cantos, a late Picasso clown... At the back of the room ATM, URL, STD, and SSN smashing a tank filled with Zip Codes, the glass cutting a digital clock-face and reminding a hitherto silent historian of Kristallnacht; others of Coventry, Guernica, Dresden.

I apologize. Please now, please don't shudder. The doctors have ordered you to recall only the best: footprints on the moon, Orville Wright's bike wheels soaring above Kitty Hawk, Jackie Robinson stealing home, the double helix, the music of pulsars and quasars.

Allow me then, a child of your middle years, to hold your hand and assure you that in whatever Valhalla dead centuries thrive, your heart will quicken. You will open all your bulging scrapbooks, display all your snapshots, explode with delight while those who preceded you gaze at your dazzling trophies. Oh, the testimonials! the endless commentaries! the crackpot prophecies! In the great festive hall you will assume head place at the table while your ancestors bow and serve you the vintage wine that has been awaiting your arrival for one hundred years. Ciao!

Deena Linett

Peace in Ireland
Ulster, January 1996

1. *Peace Talks*
Walls in Derry and Belfast declare
bright fealty, Catholic or Protestant:

Unionists swear "No Surrender" in designs
to last for an eternity, and the Virgin, roses

at the throat of her blue gown, raises
one white painted hand to bless beneath a crown

of stars. At the narrow street-end of a house,
a red-stained wall shouts *Saoirse!* What else lasts:

hills fall steep to where the loughs and wild sea
are blue, gales tear in off the Atlantic, sweep

across the swells like walls of thick green glass
before it hardens, roll between the continents

for miles and days, come home to wrap
the island in their bright irrational embrace.

In Stormont and Westminster–on the streets–
people talk to one another: seventeen months of peace.

On a morning forty days away, bombs
will blast this little quiet into history.

2. *Memories of the Root Cellar at Yaddo*
In Northern Ireland I face the sea and Rathlin Island.
Scotland, close as peace, is wrapped in fog.

Once I stood in a root cellar slumped against the earth;
through the window in its angled roof I could see

the yellow buds of branches and blue sky.
Here on hills above the sea men and women work

the wind-scoured soil to make a sanctuary,
Corrymeela, Irish Gaelic name that means *Sweet Hill:*

imagine steep roofs tenting new shoots, dormant seed
hauled and shriven in the deep vaults of the sea.

3. *News of Hostages*
In a too-hot pink hotel room in Coleraine
I watch the news: TV cameras on an island

somewhere in the south Pacific give us
driven men slouching beneath wreaths

made of leaves, absurd and necessary shade.
All Ireland's witness to the men with prods

who herd them into shameful brilliant mock parade
under palms–cousins to the palms bent by wind

at Ballycastle on the hills above the sea–
their leaves like an array of knives, sprays

of thin sharp cutting things, but green.
When the weather's clear you can see

Corrymeela: row of little wooden houses heaved
against the hills, canted roofs, steep eaves.

South Africans, like tailors fitting suits
to altered frames, came here to measure, cut and drape,

the fabric stiff beneath their hands, and strange.
Peace, like lace, is painstaking work

made by mortal hands in insufficient light. Heads bent
over the piecework, men and women pause

until the shelling stops, go on creating maps
of threads that tear and soil easily around designs

of little silver pins, and build small temporary
dwellings made of wood above the sea. Paramilitaries

leave their brothers in the cities
and come up here to put their weapons down;

at the ocean where it spits and blows
against the coast they learn a fury harder

than their own. When the wind is right
you can hear church bells: all through the night

and in dreams, their sweet sound. Let Ireland stand
for all the riven countries, let the blood

stop running on walls of bullet-chipped concrete
to puddle at the ends of narrow streets, let it flood

the places shame has covered, and the hearts
of boys and girls, their sun-warmed arms

around each other, and let them be
heavy with moisture and greed.

P.H. Liotta

On the Failure Named Bosnia

Love no country: countries soon disappear.
                              –Czeslaw Milosz

Somewhere in Hegel there is a line
    that masks the Janus truth, of how *the owl
    of Minerva flies only at dusk.* Which means,

I say, we see most wisely rearward, and so
    remain dumfounded by all that confronts us
    in the present tense. And if you read this,

Mr. President, indeed if you read
    anything any mild-spoken citizen
    has ever sent to that great house

where it seems so often no one has ever
    finished composing a thought, let
    alone a sentence, it might be worth

your time to ponder Hegel, in the dark hours
    where I understand you are given over
    to your most buried thoughts, there,

in the stillness of those corridors, where
    the ghosts of the Republic walk
    beside you. Consider how what they

have to tell you is the truth, though it may
    not be your version of it, or mine,
    or ours; but truth, nonetheless.

Some will rise as geysers of earnest passion;
    some who have sinned against the office,
    as you well know, have never repented.

A man's fate according to Heraklitos,
> is in his character. But what character
> is yours, or ours? We have all

been changed. Think of Aurelius, someone
> I know you read, when he speaks of how
> it is not death that a man should fear;

rather, it is never beginning to live.
> I respect the office, and you, if truth
> be known. But the world has gone before

our eyes. And no one, if not you, will cross
> the river of ash. The owl will fly
> into the shadow's dark soul and we will hear

only the swift whipping of a feathered wing
> crossing the moon's path. So, listen.
> Ask your guards to let you pass, alone.

Listen, tonight, when you pace the cavernous
> absence and the voices of the *Geist*
> of this Republic walk beside you.

They will tell you things you will not want
> to hear, in the carpeted silence beneath
> the dull, flickering sconce. They will call

you by name and when you hear them, do not
> turn away. Remember the clown of
> Kierkegaard, who stood at the proscenium

and announced the stage had broken into flame.
> Remember how the claque exploded
> in laughter? But what if god's clown

were real? And, absorbed through their eyes,
> we became that audience? What would we
> say when the clown's voice crackles,

fists tremble and feet smash through
> the stage? What if it were true? The theater
> is burning now. The best of us on fire.

Vyzitsa, Pelion

Timothy Liu

Billions Served

A cow without an eye? Not an uncommon sight
in stockyards run by the stocks we hold–cancer

eating out her eye, half of her face, and part
of her skull and brain. Better to have died

en route–pig sockets bleeding from electric
shocks that send them squealing down a steel sluice,

the ones not fit for meat left to starve–guts
bursting from the sides of a goat as maggots hatch

in the folds. How far now to the nearest fast-
food joint? Miles of tracks. Acres fertilized

with baby chicks ground up alive, the males no good
for hatcheries. Death's industry a sight

kept from our view where euthanasia's simply not
cost effective while the bull market rises–

a metal bolt now striking through the skulls
of newly stunned veals, conveyor belts starting up

as the hooves and heads come off whether or not
the throats are slit, finger ground down to stubs

while families try to make ends meet–
a long line of workers as far as the eye can see.

The Presence of an Absence in a Midwest Town

Crosses doused with gasoline hotter
than a mountain of books burning
on a Saturday night where ennui has
as many names as churches on the main
drag–dandelions across those lawns
with a worm curled up around each root,
the town's one signal light burnt-out.
A mother and daughter logging off
a screen left in the lap of a son
whose father was last seen cruising
Boystown. This too is America, two men

in bed reading late at night, dirt
beneath their nails as they ruminate
on a Klan Watch Report: *Nine Neo-Nazis
slay two men walking hand in hand
down a Sioux City street.* Should we
take up arms? Or vows of silence after
that order of Benedictine monks
outside Dubuque. No midnight runs
to the nearest Kum & Go without some
new threat. We deserve it, ministers
say, all of it foretold by doomsday
prophets, active Hate Groups dotting
a pull-out map of America like a field
gone wild–last year's harvest a ghost
of husks. Yet we wake each morning
to radio talk: an Anti-Smut Amendment
for children caught surfing the Net,
stiff fines imposed on porno stills
more accessible now than a single
page of the Gutenberg Bible ever was–
anyone with basic skills logging on
to get on-line with Satan (beaver shots
and dick controlled with a mouse), more
windows on those laptops than houses
still lit up this late into the night.

Edward Locke

Directing the Future

This new year shall be shot without Fellini.
    The whips and scorns
Of daydreamed husband-tyrants over many
Congenitally love-mad slaves, all thorns
Monogamy impales on, Juliet's bag
Of feudal wifely subjugation, may
Argue Fellini could conscript, conspire
With Shakespeare, but I doubt that facile tag–
Except, some weary nights both were, I'd say,
Breathed on by prostrate angels of desire;

For both, a twin afflatus seemed to hatch
    Indelicate
Asides, as if each stole the other's watch,
As if some desiccated neuron got
Their spleens in thrall, as if, at times, they spoke
In run-on tears, charred semicolons where
Fresh periods were craved. Each breathed a rose
The color of ideas. But now, the break
Arrives–death was not dubbed. The theater
Main reel is blank, though round and round she goes.

No one like them shall patch such scenes again.
    That's understood.
No one shall enter Cinecittà to gain
An eidolon with welds of gold and wood–
The cruising ship so large two thousand lights
Could not unsecret all its fogbound decks.
Paisans of Rossellini bless his sighs
Who penned their woundings to black bombers' sights;
De Sica welcomes him where bikes leave tracks–
His shoeshine urchins share their white-maned joys.

What of the midnight and its special need
    For fantasy?
That decadence Fellini makes the screed
Before resolving to integrity,
Achievement, cinematic ode–the twirl
And end of dance in fountains evening favors,
The burning creature monstrous on the pyre,
Frail blousey meadows of the spring, spa girl
In white who walks with waters, serving lovers
Where crucified shall touch the crucifier–

Denouements that give all orgied lawns
    And open veins
Their room on screen with Vitelloni dawns
Where youth sparks sex, but little else remains,
Balloons, perhaps, and memories of parades–
Then later arts, hermaphroditic tease
And gorgeous sluts in cabins in high trees.
The overwhelming tints, like masquerades
Turned riot, hide vast, wild identities.
What shall imagination do with these?

And with Fellini's loss–are we prepared
    This starry year
To come, to lose the cutting edge he dared,
The pan to caricatures born of real fear?
We must learn music that's processional,
Wherein we join at twilight the long trend
Of our filmed past: dead dads who won't stay down,
Childhood we trot behind and, lonely, call.
Now this year's eve with no wiseacre friend–
It's the last time we shall not play the clown.

Rachel Loden

Checkers Rising

Grant that the old Adam in this Child may be so
buried, that the new man may be raised up in him.
          –The Book of Common Prayer

This is the new socialist brain. This is the statue
of Dzerzhinsky falling over. This is my wife Pat.
This is an ode to the Bratsk Hydroelectric Project.
And I just want to say [abort, retry, fail...]

the kids, like all kids, love the little dog.
This/is/your/brain/speaking... So I want you all
to stonewall it. Because gentlemen, this is my last
dance contest, last waltz with Leonid

around the Winter Palace. This is the Komissar
of Moonbeams, this is the Soviet of Working People's
Reveries. This is the new man born out of Adam.
These are the new world order mysteries–oh,

Republican cloth coat. Oh gallery of Trotskyist
apostasies. Tricia and Julie do not weep for me–
I live and flourish in the smooth newt's tiny eyes,
my new brain fizzing with implanted memories.

My Night with Philip Larkin

Rendezvous with dweeby Philip in the shower:
"Aubade" taped up on pale blue tile;
I can hear him grumbling through the falling water.
Uncurling steam is scented with a trace of bile,

And I'm as grateful as a thankless child can be.
Someone has been here in this night with me,
Someone whose bitterness, I want to say,
Is even more impressive than my own.
Talking with Larkin on the great white telephone
I let the night be washed out into day

Until it's safe enough to go lie down
And dream of my librarian, my bride.
Perhaps he sits and watches in his dressing gown;
I know he won't be coming to my side
For fumblings and words he simply can't get out.
That stuff was never what it was about
When he would wake at four o'clock to piss
And part the curtains, let the moon go on
With all the things worth doing, and not done,
The things that others do instead of this.

Joan Logghe

War Crimes
dedicated to the women of Bosnia

The red ribbon used to tie the gift, and then
the child's hair, ravels. Becomes a gag.
Becomes the knot of infinity, a thing to hold
in your hand as you leave your body as spoils.

Your body becomes a piñata, a birthday vessel.
Men are hitting it blindfolded with a stick
only you are the one who can't see, and instead
of wrapped candies and treats, out spills your hair,

your breasts, eyes, shoes, and your purse full of coins
is now full of strange seed and your gifts fall
into all the hands at once. You didn't want to share,
not this. A thing once known as pain crosses over

from feeling into shock. And a slight slap unhinges
what is left of a moon. And silent. Torn scarf,
rapid water, and a rip tide, all in body. Dense salt,
a bucket of roses rises in your throat

and you start a long scream. If Bosnian women sang,

a red ribbon would rise out of their mouths and
find its way around the necks of the men, unsacred,
whose fingers smell of iron, breath, brute as poison.

Nobody wants to dwell in the basement of torture,
lift their skirt to try and find the soprano. Screams
are not opera. Screams tumble out of cave mouths, wind
is their relative, a natural force like tornado.

When I gave birth, the best part was being kin
to all women who opened their legs and thighs, pushed
out a head and loved it. Every human I met became my son.
Every face fell back into newborn. When ravished

what can you do but rise? No further place to fall, your own
discovery of gravity. If the women were given back
their clothes and threads for mending, would they sew
the fingers of rapists to their cocks? Lips to hats?

Attack is a pattern of chaos and rapid fire
ugly. Homilies read like the whistles of wolves.
Or would they mend? Add extra embroidery, the stitch
called compassion stitch, French knots, red and blue roses.

I write from my comfort, an offer to carry something
holy and heavy. You show me your blue plate, the only
artifact left of your home. We strain into each other,
our bodies insulated with fiberglass batt of distance.

I have no sister. Call you sister, hand you a ribbon.
Tie back your beautiful, profaned hair, a Guernica
of pain on your face, a hosanna of hope. If words have power,
suck articulation back inside. After war, words must suffice.

Jeffrey Loo

For Etheridge Knight
1931–March 10, 1991

Break–heart, in your madness–
rejoice in nothing that is–tomorrow's
the day Etheridge goes down deeper than sleep–
he's gone out today like thin air–
his life-force breath and spirit freed
from the poor tortured body in disease

will never sing again—
what garbage this world is—
heaped up plastic circuit lies
and foam-rubber elastics
stinking like deaths that cannot be
without what you sing—
Mississippi blues and mosquito rivers run
and carry you miles like the speaking drum
mantra of flesh–bone–skin–tones–

    ...your echo calls me, then as now
to say to them what you told me—
but the no-good Nile and ravaged Hudson run
like bodies of glass
bearing industrial mass—
without your breathing voice anymore
the trees crack like old factory panes
and the leaves bleed through black acid holes
made by chemical rainfalls—
the inhuman moon loves no one anymore...
Old friend—for the spirit of the wood,
for the beauty that made you immortal
for the end—the speaking
and the hearing drums pound us all
away into the tongue of purest sound—
poet of soul-blues/jazz and song
I know too well how I miss you now,
first sayer of the sooth-said psalm that gave
my voice liberty to swing
when you said: "Just SAY a poem..."
and I heard your echoing power
in each thing of this life-world...

    And now all night in tiny pieces I remember
how much hope and strength you lent me,
your voice deep and gentle as explosions under sea
as oral wisdom humbles hyper literacy,
I heard your South with awe,
your America a horror show of laws—
you knew all along how heady poets jam
images like waters pushing over a dam
(and it AIN'T got that swing
to mean any DAMNED meaning thing)–

how poems for the page are aimed
into linear ages that never arrive–
their futures never mature into *now*–

    Speaker of truths–
what else can you be?...
Sainthood's too high
and prisons make a faith of abuse–
You believed in your self enough to open the deep
and sweet cells of the heart even in ruins
no one could bear–your voice like a thunderhead
made so many leaves tremble
to answer your gale with words–
So many times you started over from scratches
deep enough to kill ten men–
I hear your grasp of hungry pain,
its pulsing rhyme of clash
like ragtime tiger pianos–
there every note strikes–hammering bone–

    The world becomes criminally insane
without you beating its cinder-block walls–
without your refraining voice
ringing out what must be–
telling/tolling to become
all you survived–transformed
creating glories from agonies–
but terrible beauties *free*-born,
music of the mired-shit of foreign wars,
so crises/politics/presidents
become no lies, no liars, but resonance–
a triumph no next wind can unhinge,
your greatness pouring melody
to and from what never changes
and changes every thing...
Faithful to the abuses of these killing times,
you lynch the stone-deaf denial in us all,
you string up love's pain with laughter
piercing your own heart–
the first act of love...

    You make milk-toast critics cringe
as if human experience had reached *in*–
as if your experience were *also* human–

like Gwendolyn Brooks asked about universality:
"Isn't black experience part of the universe?"
But the harmony of this universe
is part ripped out now,
and only remembering you, without you–
yet your soul can sing:
so my soul can sing...

I didn't know till this moment
there was anyone who'd make me cry
      by just dying–
I'd forgotten how to remember love
till this moment
      of breaking–
I thought I was hollow as a chime
but at this touch my space
      is screaming
out of the blues into the brackish
white-water and the black
      sea of you–

Etheridge,
Take heart in your madness–
Rejoice–even when there's
nothing to fill the spaces
women leave behind in the air
when they're gone–
Rejoice even when you say
"What's the *use* of talking to myself
when I've heard it all before?"
Rejoice–because the heart
is mad for liquid joy–
and *asking* what love is
makes loving into retrospecting–
In the air you left for me
the space is my own palm
now pressed like a seashell
telling its roar–
Rejoice–fires burn only the cold.
One wave follows its brother,
and till I see you as another, *Rejoice...*

Susan Luther

Hymn for the Children of Israel
Yitzhak Rabin 1917-1995
Blessed are the peacemakers, for they
shall be called the children of Gad.

Soon, terror in Jerusalem.

And now, here, in the "safe"
USA: even children
are killing their teachers.

Blackboard cleaning solvent in a teacup.
A gun: aimed for all

eliminating one, and the life
of a stray girl of fourteen.

   –Harvest, November, the time
   for Thanksgiving: naked

and barren

though anyone, though history
may be. Though *Kaddish* has been sung for one

all the world ought to be mourning:

   Another father has died
   Another mother, another son.

   Another leader, another

dream: though Israel has seen

fall a *Grandfather,*
peacemaker, zeal
by zeal tumbled down:

oh praise then, praise yes
to *extremis* justice for all

our fine dead would have craved for us, all–though nothing is all
we can hope for–

we ever have: *Sparrow-thrum at the empty*
feeder. Black rhombus of a crow. Coffee so thick & old
who else

would drink it, *red* cactus
red red red weeks before
Christmas, sweet smell
of the wash, towel-scent
in the fold. The tears,
soul–debt

of one good man: oh praise him, the blade

in your hand (whiff of garlic
on skin) scraping fiber
from stalk, for weeks stilled: surrender
and striving–Carolina wren
trilling a heartbeat away on the sill.

Rick Lyon

Venice, Easter 1996: In Memory of Joseph Brodsky

It's not bad, Joseph–the city you loved,
the place I've finally arrived and long dreamed of–not bad.
Stepping from the train to find the main road into town's water and
    traveled by boat,
reassured, almost, to know what's under one's feet is always moving,
passing the facades of palazzi, crumbling and restored,
the push of an oar propelling a gondola,
while the overcast sky thankfully filters the sunlight.
High up on a building whose windows are barred with iron grates–
    a former prison, maybe–
I saw my first of the many Venetian lions of St. Mark,
the lion with wings which holds a book, a copy of the Bible,
the symbol of Venice, the one you chose, which might've chosen you,
who traveled so far from your homeland
and whose poems sank deep into your countrymen's hearts.
All the bells of San Marco ringing together–their gongs and clangs–
are like a resounding voice which captures our inner selves.
Many of the people in the bustling piazza stop to listen, wonderstruck.
While the grandeur and Renaissance splendor of the city must've
    pleased you,
I guess you loved the water the best
in this too romantic place where one might easily fall in love.
At night, the gondolas stationed along the quay rock and slap the water
    in their berths,

while the fleet of steel-hulled vaporettos, rafted together, slam into one
    another with a *boom*
and the well-worn paving stones, crowded in the daytime, are crossed by
    a solitary cat.
The long line of yellow lights marks the channel across the lagoon,
where late-night riders stand silhouetted on the boats ferrying them home.
They look back to the shore, at the people still strolling along the waterfront
where groups of boys while away the evening
and the domes and campaniles stand in sharp relief.
The grandeur of the city balances that of the sea
and brings an equilibrium in which one might rest.
On the bridge I lean over, there's a carving of the welcoming lion,
his paw extended, holding his book.

Don Mager

The Unbearable Truth that Is Beauty

In Ankara, Elizabeth Taylor[1] stands in white hair.
    She solicits for Chechen orphans–
        her own voice almost orphaned,
        like a girl's plaintive allure.

A golf ball sized tumor, grown onto her brain, has been cut
    out. Have we not been watching her now
        most of our lives? Is she not
        what, in its extravagance,

we call beauty? For beauty is only performance, a
    taking of oneself out of oneself
        to be a thing more perfect,
        more resplendent and simple.

Like grief beauty is a role larger than those who act it.
    But, is not her voice, its girl shyness,
        an attempt to withdraw
        from the terrible burden

of such ravishment? And has not her misery of
    men become our myth too? Our desire?

---

[1] The description refers to Ms. Taylor's first public appearance (late July 1997) after the removal of a benign tumor in her brain.

          Might we be loved—loved
             also and sheltered—despite
what we are. Might an Orpheus lead us into life and
        not look back. And each time we shatter
            ourselves in hunger, do we
            not want to be brides again
too, as if the gift of beginning were never used up?
        Like a fierce violence in the mind
            she is what acting is–a
            line crossed into deception,
moments of blazing triumph, and the falling back from them.
        We are our own singularities
            most fully at the instant
            we open like stargazer
lilies and become, unflinchingly before a strong sun,
        a body more achieved than we could
            know how to be: dancer in
            his flight, or runner cutting
air with her breath, or lover on his unspent, spending and
        unspendable crest. If we were not
            able to stand up in white hair
            and speak out in a small girl's
orphaned voice, to impersonate, to show, would we ever
        be wanted? Behind the display, she
            shrinks. Before it we spend
            ourselves in amazement.
And now as the gazers and the gazed upon grow older,
        our separate golf balls fester, grown past
            cutting out. They have become
            us. Wounder and wound are one.

James Magner

Ritual of the Green
for Stanley Kunitz

I can see you now
in the green labyrinth of your years,
become, again, the ancient child of earth.

For to there, beneath the sea of voices,
communing eyes and tongues,
of all your yesterdays
is where your heart has cried to be
–even through evening and unfolding love
of words with sons at table,
even through blood-filled diaphany,
resonance of audience and students,
communicants with your sacred orchestration,
it all has moved
as a river of your heart's flow,
to where you are now
with your coiled and braided friends of Eden
and the culminating Green
of your sacrament of Life,
beneath the stars,
become one, now, with the sun
and the spirit of the gentle dead
that are always ours
in dying into heart
beyond the mind
–one song, now, one triumph, one rest
in green lips, now, lisping light
–O Resolution
of all dissonance and the dark,
the miracle and communion,
the bright and single life, now,
of son become the father
and of the farthest, most intimate
regions of the heart
in the deft, most gentle, touch
of fingers to the innocent and staring earth.

Mordecai Marcus

The Enduring Poet: Farewell to Stephen Spender

His star-fraught words infused the stuff of dream
Into low aspirations of our flesh
Until its frightened breathing cleared the stream
Where song lures touch into a common mesh.

He sang how fortitude and loneliness
Can interinanimate the hero's reach
And with a grave timidity to bless
He forged great prayers from unsacred speech.

As wars refluxed, he cursed their futile blast.
As song grew harsh, he took its measure fairly.
He treasured births and echoes from the past
Although at last he added to them sparely,

And if his weak words splinter a far bell
His best are whole, no ghost nor torsoed marble.

Charles Martin

Stanzas after *Endgame*

1.
    Hurrying off toward a tiny Off-Off-Off-
    Off-Broadway theater on the Bowery,
    We step around a shouting match of gruff
        Derelicts whose poverty
    This Sunday afternoon has found a small
Stage to enact its outrage on, a temporary
    Refuge from the wrecker's ball;

2.
    Here artists and their lofts survive by grace
    Of our needy city's celebrated
    Developers, whose greed for office space
        Seems for now to have abated;
    And here men wait with rags and dirty water
To smear new grime on windshields of intimidated
    Drivers who curse, but give a quarter;

3.
    Quarters accumulated to buy a quart
    Of *Gold Coin Extra* or *Lone Star Malt Brew*;
    Others do crack or heroin, or snort
        Fumes out of bags of plastic glue;
    In the urinous storefronts where they meet,
Nodding acquaintances impatiently renew
    The ties that bind them to the street.

4.
    No better place than this to stage a play
    That illustrates the way the world will end,
    For who will come to see it anyway,
        But the subscribers, who attend
    Everything? Yet look: pressed against the curb's
Split lip, twin arks—from which, in disbelief descend
    Dazed voyagers from distant suburbs:

5.
    Two *Short Line* buses with the audience:
    The first is full of high school kids and teachers,
    The second carries senior citizens
        Clutching discount ticket vouchers;
    As they negotiate front stairs and aisle,
Purplespiked mutants grimly stalk the blue-rinsed grouches
    Up and into the theater, while

6.
    We in the middle find our seats and pray,
    Unhopefully, that Beckett's precision
    Survive all cries of "What did he just say?"
        And adolescent snorts of derision:
    The young with their tongues in one another's ears,
And their elders talking back to television,
    Except this isn't television, dears.

7.
    The lights go down and we become aware
    Of someone on stage, motionless at first,
    Beginning to move around a covered chair;
        The way taken is at once reversed:
    Upstage, downstage, dithering left and right,
Until the tiny stage is thoroughly traversed:
    No other characters in sight.

Katherine McAlpine

Yellow Submarine Homesick Blues Revisited

For sixties veterans this is *déjà vu:*
a two-day crafts and music celebration–
feathers, face-painting booths and *temps perdu*

in a cow field uncowed for the occasion.
The now well-over-thirty generation
hasn't yet totally chilled out. See here
diehard survivors of the Woodstock Nation
recalling the tambourines of yesteryear.

Don't look too closely and it's like old days:
a tent pitched here, a red VW bus
parked there, a jug band, miles of macramé.
But something's different from the way it was.
The cops who've come to keep the peace for us
all look about sixteen. Sweet Jesus, we're
so old, we're even older than the fuzz!
Recalling the tambourines of yesteryear

are mimes and jugglers on a makeshift stage,
grassy aromas from the parking lot.
I don't smoke anymore. It must be age:
no high. I just cough three times and pass out.
I see a number of torsos gone to pot,
though (too many soy croquettes or too much beer?),
and lunch austerely on alfalfa sprouts,
recalling the tambourines of yesteryear.

Serene earth moms in patchwork peasant skirts
inspect the weaving and the pottery.
Their adolescent daughters, sullen flirts
with hacked-off neon hair, would rather be
home watching Madonna prance on MTV
and hate their names. I count one Guinevere,
two Stars, three Rainbows and a Harmony,
recalling the tambourines of yesteryear

till finally the sun sets in a Day-Glo
orange blaze. Escaped balloons and kites
roost in the trees. Small children fret as they grow
sticky and tired; strayed dogs reunite
with owners; fiddles pierce the fading light.
Graying ex-hippies gather up their gear
and boogie gently into that good night,
recalling the tambourines of yesteryear.

Rebecca McClanahan

Writers' Conference, Last Dance

It writhes and bumps, grinds
        its hundred feet into the floor, antennae arms
                rising, one beast of flesh and musk breathing its single
                      breath, this animal we make together larger
                than any of us alone–the young girl in haiku,
        her brief skirt banding a muscular rump
(so much to say in such a small space),
the experimental novelist whispering

his many voices into the ear of the lyrical
        poet whose long lines are breaking
                like waves around his neck while the journalist,
                      invisible in the center of things, flings
                his arms into the air. In the corner an editor,
        all legs and black sheath, dances with herself,
    has been dancing like this all night, patiently
noting the scholar partnered by a cane.

Beneath trousers and dresses, old hamstrings strum,
        burn scars of envy tighten and recede, stockings
                web our spider veins, push-up forms lift us
                      to a higher place or take the place
                of what's been taken. It's late, and we are not
        as we were when the dance began,
    or as my aunt once said, leaping in sprung
rhythm from her bed beside the dead

clock–*Oh my! It's later than it's ever been!*
        Last song, last frenzy of tentacles and centipedal
                fury, high heels skittering, sneakers squealing,
                      the clomp of boots, the occasional bare foot
                risking it all as we fly momentarily
        up and out of our selves–hurry, already
    we are splitting, already breaking apart in midair–
one pulse thumping, one heart beating fierce.

David B. McCoy
From *The Oil War: 1991*

Day 10
From television news broadcasts
I learn the new total number
of successful sortie missions
allied forces have flown over
Iraq and Kuwait. To date, over twenty
thousand–dropping more bomb tonnage
than that dropped on all of Japan.
But having learned a fatal lesson
from the media coverage
of the Vietnam War, Army
Intelligence experts release
only a few flashy game-like
videos of night-time bombing
runs–being careful never to show
what must be horrendous damage. Even
the language of this war is quaint:
"Bombing missions" are now "sortie
missions;" the "battlefront" is now
the "theater of operations;"
"killing the enemy" has become just
"neutralizing the enemy."
To gain at least some perspective
of what destruction there must be,
I slide from under my desk a
box containing family papers
and World War II photographs my
father sent back from Nagasaki.
The scenes are familiar
to most–a city leveled to
ruins. But one photo, always
the last, shows a man with his mouth
wide open in what must have been
his final scream as flesh was blown
from his body in one great flash.
Perhaps if there were some stead-fast,
clear-cut reason for declaring
war on Iraq, instead of all
those superficial reasons given

by President Bush (which seem to
change as regularly as the phases
of the moon), I would not feel in
my gut the wreckage of all those bombs.

Walt McDonald

Once You've Been to War

There are times when everything I touch
turns to leaves, my plot of earth breathing
like women who seem to be always fertile,
their nurseries teeming with mouths,
flower-print dresses forever bulging.

Whatever I plant at night in dreams
by dawn has rooted, ferns like veils,
orchids, fuchsia tendrils reaching for trees,
my secret back yard dense as the front,
three canopies of rain forest

chattering with spider monkeys,
toucans, orange and black minahs,
birds of paradise. And there are times
deep in my pillow below three canopies
of rain forest I did not plant

but helped to burn, the sand bags burst
and sand blows over everything.
Concertina wire can't hold it back.
Roaches blue-bronzed and emerald,
the size of condors,

tweezer their way over dunes
the winds shuffle and fold like cards.
Rockets slam down beyond the trees,
fall-out clatters the leaves
like hail. In parched riverbeds

fish keep flopping,
jets diving are lightning without rain,
and in the distance, bombs explode so long
the hollows of my knees flutter
like flutes whittled from bone.

The War in Bosnia

Mast snapped in half, this family wagon like a tank
crashes embankments of daily tasks, flag flapping in slush
up to the hub, gun turret splattered with mud.
Our son and others roar real tanks through snow-packed
mine fields in Bosnia. More soldiers train under flags
at Fort Carson, as he did, dodging blizzards and snakes,
the Rockies snow-capped, far from us trapped on flat plains,
slapping the family wagon through maddening traffic

back to our house where we pace the screened back porch
and watch the news, thankful for the mail,
even TV. We rock on the worn plank porch
and watch the sun go down, pace zig-zag lines
across the boards, thinking about trails
and fields where our son's tank roars, a million mines.

Robert McGovern

Of Military Scandals
after Diego Velazquez's *Mars*, c. 1636-42

If only we could do this to all arms-bearers, all warriors: laugh at them. It would be the end of wars, as nobody could raise the energy to fight when everybody thinks they are hilariously funny.... [He] slumps here, brooding and melancholy, his armour useless around him and the only thing still erect is his moustache.
–Sister Wendy Beckett

Vulcan, tipped by the tattletale poet-god,
snared in a brazen net the four-star lover
bedded with his wife (she of the shell-half),
surprising the lovers' Olympic grapple, and called
the deities to eye the thrashing pair.

Venus escaped the rumpled bed before
the easel focused the warrior's riant shame
and chiaroscuro could show his fractured state—
the man in the golden helmet, were he else not naked,
helmet serving to shade his pouting eyes;
his bulging biceps, thighs, and calves bespeak
a life of violent action, as opposed to the smithy
(in the artist's painting of the cuckolding's revelation)
with powerful arms and legs and honest torso,
unwrinkled as it is with the war-god's loss of face

(whose pose bespeaks the absurdity of one
caught playing with something other than the pole
he seems to fondle underneath the drape),
and who probably forged the useless marshal's arms
beside the bed, late scene of valiant thrust.

The sullen god, baroquely diapered in drape,
bemoans his now mere limpid lust revealed
and the probable loss of his bloody high command.

Ella
(1918-1996)
Fitzgerald

Celtic by name who grew
a Mayv
of the ten-inch 78, where blues
could segue on the flip to the joy
of moon at apogee–
no time in song for tragedy.

Love comes in three minute spells,
and pain's as quick, gathered up
in a brown and yellow basket–
no time in jazz for anything but life.

Gutsy Mayv knew her Mack the Knife,
but love and laughter scored her nights and days–
no time in life for anything but joy.

Though you lost your eyes, legs, long life,
you phrase and scat us still
and laser-live,

our deity of song.

Peter Meinke

Greenhouse Statistics

Four hundred and fifty azaleas
ring our home: a dollhouse dusted
by butterflies   Four hundred we planted
one by delicate one for three decades
cuttings from the original thirty

This perfumed cornucopia spills
ninety-five yards from Big Bayou
where Tampa Bay gapes on the Gulf of Mexico
whose waters rise dark and sure as the shadow
of doom four feet every hundred years
because we love our sweet machines
more than life itself and bring
on rain for us and dust for Northerners:
the good Lord's sense of humor we presume

Our front step stands ten feet above
sea level giving the house they've
just told us   two hundred years to go
We should feel safe and yet
impermanence blooms like plaque in the teeth
of our resolve   To rake the lawn
to dig up roots and rocks to sand
window frames and oil the locks
seem somehow not worth it if it all
comes to wreckage in the end   Biblical
prophecies whirl about our heads
drought and flood and famine and disease
gallop in the distance inching toward us
like relentless locusts from the Holy Land

and high above our quiet town
fly Air Force jets with God knows what
payload that could engulf us all
wood and stone marrow and bone
My sweetest dear with whom I've labored
on this house for thirty years
how can we kiss apocalypse?
Because we can imagine our children's
children's children this is no distant
burning out of sons but family
tragedy as palpable as Robert
drowning in Frenchman's Creek or pretty
cousin May who left for school
one day and never came home again

Or shouldn't we think about these children
yet to be just hold together as we hold
together now planting azaleas that

outlive us fixing the house because
we love it ignoring the water lapping
at our feet? Recycle cans refusing plastic
bags? Embrace our children on the holidays
lugging out the albums once again
to laugh at what we looked like "way
back when" fondly recalling pets
now long since dead? But we're not cats
and dogs: looking ahead we'll build
a boat and teach our children's children
how to swim and do the dead man's float

Assisted Living

At the adult center we hunch
like mechanical spores
on the ground floor hallway
outside the arthritic elevator
our chrome appendages clanking
and hooking each other as we stuff
ourselves into the box and turn around

Language is queer: adult movies
mean fucking but adult center
means dying though both mean
without dignity in front of others
In the elevator our spotted hands
and heads shake like mushrooms in rain

Not one in here but hasn't had
adventure We have cried out
in bed and staggered home at midnight
Proud and passionate we have made
terrible mistakes and paid for them

or not: it makes no difference Life
a gravity stew irresistible everything
dragged under together: the sparkiest eye
the sly hand the delicate breast

If there were humor left in this small band
it would raise its drying voice and shout
knowing most are deaf: *Going down!*

But no one says a word and we wait
fungily for someone to smush

a button

Gregory McNamee

Sarasvati in the New World

Solipsistic, blinking, wander
trembling, mindless, through whitewashed archways
and jade curves of chacmools,
among hyacinth, turquoise, birds of paradise,
amid the annihilating fire,
the obliterated past. Envision
Haida, Menomenee, Cashinahua, Tukano,
Kayapo, Cakchiquel, Bororo, Tillamook,
Modoc, Wampanoag, Gê, Chiricahua,
Vizcaina and Tuatha dé Danann.
Try to locate a history
that has been disappeared.
Every one of us is a foreigner now.

In the New World a new millennium
arises to erase whatever has come before it.
Two thousand nails in a splintered cross,
minus six and counting, two thousand
brads carved of jade, and a rose far away
in Jericho. Who among us may gather it?

See the rose spread in Casasola's faces,
in the mummified newborns of Guanajuato,
in the murdered plowmen of Salvador,
in the open eyes of *los desaparecidos,*
in the supple noise of mountain water,
in new leather, flour cakes, raw diesel,
and dooryards full of fighting cocks
clawing at petals.
Who truly believes he has mastered these?
What, generals, is left to be commanded?

A rose in Jericho, but time ends,
and the earth plants its sweet flowers
in the boneyards of the Americas,

in the ribcages of conquistadores.
Take the black glass from its heart.
Spin it northward to dying seas,
spin it southward to dying forests,
the wounded houses of infinity.
Spin it over countless nations.
Spin it until it melts into gold.

Two thousand nails, and Sarasvati trembles
within the mouth of all eternity,
within the eyes of mythless continents.
She sings an air from the Río de la Plata
of dancing mothers and screaming jets.
She shapes a bit of bone from Chile.
She smooths a pyramid of emeralds
and zacuan feathers, endlessly.

A cataract of new blood thunders
from red-tiled rooftops everywhere.
A hundred million flowers wither.
Sarasvati, mother of all we will never see,
Athena, mother of our emptiness,
Nuestra Señora, blessed trinity,
none among us can know why you ever smiled.
Foreigners, we walk between gates of flame.
Where now are the ears to hear our prayers?
Who can live within a wall of fire?

Jean Monahan

Dolly

On February 22, Ian Wilmut stunned the world by announcing that he and his team at the Roslin Institute outside Edinburgh had created an exact copy—a clone—of an adult Dorset sheep. The historic lamb was named Dolly.
　　–*Business Week,* March 1997

When she kneels on the tattered straw
to wrangle her mother's teat,
burrowing into the familiar fleece
stuck with buffs and feces,
she hears, in the dumb throb of her heart,
the lashing waves of the great flood
that hammered the narrow planks of the hold
where the first lamb hunkered

between a lioness and an ox.

In a world tamed and ordered
by difference, she is more of the same,
one too many. The ark rocks
with the mutiny of her birth.

She does not question, as we must,
the possibility of repeating only the best
of ourselves, endlessly.

The black line around his gold haunch.
The full throat. The right waltz.

Deep night on the coast,
the villagers shift into a collective dream
of hailstorms and plagues of birds.
Tomorrow they will learn of Dolly's birth,
she who will take away
the sins of the world.
Overhead, the moon echoes
her mother's eye,
shining slyly, waning and widening.

Michael Mott

In Memory of William Stafford
1914-1993

Ten minutes before dark
the swan flies down the lake
over the wine-dark autumn water
toward the dam and rush of water,
its wings tic-tac, its body
one line of white from beak
to feet. As Edward Thomas wrote:
"As if the bow had flown off
with the arrow."

That doe and unborn fawn
cleared from the mountain road
in Oregon have reached the
bottom of the canyon, and in
the prairie farmhouse, two

hundred miles from anywhere
on earth, the telephone
rings, rings, and now
no one on earth will answer.

Joan Murray

Taking the Count

1.
Tonight a soldier is taking photos
on the highway north of Al Jahrah, Kuwait.
He will pass them around
when he's back home, will show his wife
though maybe not his children–but certainly
the men who teach with him at school,
and later some of the neighbors–
maybe when it's summer
and they're sitting around the pool,
so they can see how many
arms and legs are sticking out,
and can imagine how many there were,
and a thousand tons of fire pounding down,
and the way the earth shook.

2.
Tonight a student is standing in the lights
of a patrol car at the University of Rochester.
He has a can of paint and has left
ten thousand small white marks
on the steps of the university library–
not knowing yet (as no one does) that there are
a hundred thousand–maybe a hundred
and fifty thousand–to the count.
He is being read his rights,
he is being patted down for weapons,
he is being shoved into the back seat of the car
to be driven to the station–
to be charged "with a defacement
that will take forever to erase."

3.
Tonight a priest is picking his way across the sand
that flanks the road to As Salman, Iraq.
He is stopping here and there, and one by one,
scratches out a work of mercy.
The shovel in his hands
might have spread manure
on the charred fields
beyond their burned villages,
or might have helped them probe for water
in this winter drought,
but tonight, though uncertain of their rituals,
he is building little mounds–
since there's no way left but this one
to be merciful.

Carol Muske

To the Muse
New Year's Eve, 1990

She danced topless, the light-eyed drunken girl
who got up on the bow of our pleasure boat
last summer in the pretty French Mediterranean.

Above us rose the great gray starboard flank
of an aircraft carrier. Sailors clustered
on the deck above, cheering, and the caps rained down,

a storm of insignia: U.S.S. *Eisenhower*.
I keep seeing the girl when I tell you
the *Eisenhower*'s now in the Gulf, as if

the two are linked: the bare-breasted dancer
and a war about to be fought. Caps fell
on the bow and she plucked one up, set it rakishly

on her red hair. In the introspective manner
of the very drunk, she tipped her face dreamily up,
wet her lips, an odalisque, her arms crossed

atop the cap. Someone, a family member, threw a shirt
over her and she shrugged it off, laughing, palms
fluttering about her nipples. I tell you I barely knew

those people, but you, you liked the girl, you
liked the ship. You like to fuck, you told me.
The sex of politics is its intimate divisive plural,

we, us, ours. *Who's over there?* You ask—*not us*.
Your pal is there, a flier stationed on a carrier.
He drops the jet shrieking on the deck. Pitch dark:

he lowers the nose toward a floating strip of
lit ditto marks and descends. Like writing haiku—
the narrator is a landscape. A way of staying subjective

but humbling the perceiver: a pilot's view.
When you write to your friend I guess that
there are no margins, you want him to see

everything you see and so transparent is
your kind bravado: he sees that too. Maybe
he second-guesses your own desire to soar over

the sand ruins, sit yourself in the masked pit
and rise fifteen hundred screaming feet a minute
into an inaccessible shape: falcon, hawk—Issa's

blown petals? Reinvent war, then the woman's faithless
enslaved dance. Reinvent sailors bawling at the rail
and the hail of clichés: flash of legs on the slave deck.

Break the spell, reverse it: caps on the waves as they
toss away their uniforms, medals, stars. Then the girl
will wake up, face west, a lengthening powerful figurehead

swept gold with fire. The waves keep coming: the you, the me,
the wars. Here is the worst of it, stripped, humiliated—
or dancing on the high deck, bully-faced, insatiable.

Here is the lie that loves us as history personified,
here's the personification: muse, odalisque, soldier,
nightfall—swear to us, this time, you will make it right.

Field Trip

Downtown, on the precinct wall,
hang the maps of Gang Territories,
blocks belonging to the red Bloods
or blue Crips. Colored glass hatpins

prick out drive-by death sites–
as the twenty-five five-year olds
pass by. They hold each other's hands
behind their tour guide, a distracted

man, a sergeant, speaking so far over
their heads, the words snap free
of syntactical gravity: *perpetrator,
ballistic.* The kids freeze in place,

made alert by pure lack of comprehension.
Then, like the dread Med fly, they specialize:
touching fingerprint pads and then their faces,
observing the coffee machine (the plastic cup

that falls and fills in place), the laser printer
burning in the outlines of the Most Wanted
beneath a poster of a skeleton shooting up.
It's not so much that they are literal minds

as minds literally figurative: they inquire
after the skeleton's health. To them a thing
well imagined is as real as what's out the window:
that famous city, city of fame, all trash and high

cheekbones, making itself up with the dreamy paints
of a First Stage Alert. The sergeant can't help
drawing a chalk tree on the blackboard. He wants
them to see that Justice is a metaphor, real as you

and me. Where each branch splits from the trunk,
he draws zeros and says they're fruit, fills each
with a word: arrest, identification, detention,
till sun blinds the slate. Not far away, through

double-thick glass, a young man slumps
on a steel bench mouthing things, a clerk
tallies up personal effects. Now he comes
to the gangs, how they own certain colors

of the prism, indigo, red–he doesn't tell
how they spray-paint neon FUCKS over
the commissioned murals. The kids listen
to the story of the unwitting woman

gunned down for wearing, into the war zone,
a sunset-colored dress. She was mistaken
for herself: someone in red.
She made herself famous, the way people

do here, but unconsciously—becoming
some terrible perfection of style,
(bordering as it does, on threat.)
The sergeant lifts his ceramic mug,

etched with twin, intertwining hearts,
smiling like a member of a tribe. Later,
on the schoolroom floor, the kids
stretch out, drawing houses with chimneys,

big-headed humans grinning and waving
in lurid, non-toxic crayon. Here is
a policeman, here a crook. Here's a picture
of where I live, my street, my red dress.

                Our planet, moon. Our sun.

Mildred J. Nash

An Invitation of Sorts

Look how the full moon keeps
an image of the sun reflecting back
all night–calling us out to moonbathe in
spring's delicately light caprice!
Falling half-moons blossoming again
surround us as we walk the city streets
where tree-topped lamplight leaps

in imitation moonlight.
Blown by an April breeze and whim–its human
counterpart–we find ourselves at last
where we can see the latest light:
Hale-Bopp's frozen fire linking past
to unimagined future times which lapse
as we bask in its light.

Capriccioso comet!
Head with its hair standing on end! You jolt
earth into love with heaven! Intersecting

strands of time and space that set
us briefly outside time and space, you spark
imagination's brightest fire. The wind
picks up–it must suspect

we've scared our scarcity
of vision, opened up new avenues
to speculation–night, an enterprise
encouraging the mystery
that somehow in the scheme of things there lies
a clever crafter–maybe more than one!
If only we could see

how brightness makes us blind–
how light blocks out what lies beyond the dark!
But we grow bored and bid Hale-Bopp goodbye,
turn back–retrace our steps to find
as many lights on earth as in the sky.
The full moon now hangs almost overhead
and nothing's left behind.

John Frederick Nims

Moses Descending

The burning questions of our time? They're burning,
That's all, as Troy did once. The ashes stay.
It's not with such concern our hearts are churning:
What moves the star by night, the sun by day
hints at a primal *Why?* beyond the headlines,
Beyond the mole-eyed scientist's surmise.
Fiercer than any hunger in the breadlines,
To know! to know! is the hunger in our eyes.

But how? In a world by glutes and cleavage haunted,
Horoscope, crystal, junk bonds, fads and trends,
Gospel on T-shirts, string bikinis flaunted
To "make a statement." Moses, lo! descends,
Waves plastic tablets with gilt lettering:
"Good is what feels good, people. Do your thing!"

D. Nurkse

Payless

The panhandler who knew my name
lies covered with a blue wool blanket,
the doorway where he slept
sealed with a strip of tape–
–a barrier a sparrow could pass:

two plainclothes write in notebooks,
each listening to a different radio:

I'll give my quarter instead
to the girl who waits at Payless,
who rocks on her heels in a dream,
only a paper cup placed carefully
outside the ring of frozen urine
to show she's still asking.

Francis O'Connor

The Venerable Tree

Several weeks ago, in the midst of a construction project...a truck knocked the limb off a tree [revealing] a six inch tall ivory statue of the Virgin Mary... embedded in the trunk of the tree.... Whatever the statue's origins, it made the tree an object of great interest and veneration on [East] 71st Street. People have adorned the tree with flowers, prayers, mass cards, bells, and candles. The bottom of the trunk is clad everywhere with rosary beads....
    –Ed McCoyd," 'Miracle' on 71st St: 'Madonna' Tree Venerated,"
    Our Town, New York, October 21, 1990

This is an odd neighborhood:
Manhattan's "East Side"–Yorkville–
(Yuppyville)–silk-stocking-ville–
where museums and hospitals flourish,
limousines gridlock, and the discrete rich
discreetly reside in maisonette,
townhouse, condo, co-op (even rentals),
while the canny beggar on Madison Avenue
solicits a C-note–and gets one a day.

The sun, of course, shines each day
first on the patron class–and sets
on the "West Side," where creative types
(mostly lit and music), migrate
from villages below 14th

to be near the Natural History museum
and Broadway's extended cowpath North
to Columbia and The Cloisters. Over here,
land is "marked" as unnatural "history."

Such is the myth of the place–displacing
what only police and priests know:
that somewhere between rich and homeless,
behind the secret tenement windows
that look to the sides of avenues,
lurks that tension of craft and lore,
taut as a gene's mnemonic spring,
of the old country's worshiping
at shrines deep beneath the cathedrals–

where the world-tree clutched earth,
miming sacrificial leaves
bared to heaven's scathing sight–
where sacraments echoed rites
only outcasts dared recall–
where, childless, you sought the crone–
lame, the forest's hornèd elf–
and the priest himself, knowing grace,
left God to the gods, and beat his bell....

SO: when the truck rammed the tree
and smashed its limb, they found an icon
in the splintered wound–and worshiped
this pearl without price–this bolt
of memory that renewed today,
redeemed the rosary's tedium,
the mass' rote, and spoke to souls
that saw the injured tree upturned:
crown to hell–roots at prayer.

Jamie O'Halloran

No Angel
Oklahoma City, Spring 1995

Blasted apart the building falls together, holds
children and workers among its shuffled decks.
The fleece of insulation clumps into shrouds,
some washed uncommonly red. What was hidden

now hides the new dead. Everything's confused:
the bodies, a child's sneaker, the president's portrait
snug to a wall. Doors swing and moan in the Spring weather,
their lintels smeared with wrong blood and too late
for the passing over. Our dead are counted by weeks,
their numbers rising with the days' searching hours.
They are carried on the arms of strong men into the light,
the light we turn from into the deep and emptying tomb.

Adrian Oktenberg

Hyakutake

The star returns and pierces once, here,
just at the tail-end of winter, at the anniversary
of my mother's death. It would seem that God,
sitting in Her blackened sky, surrounded
by the seraphim stars, acknowledges this
by sending the messenger Comet Hyakutake.
But no. God died, circa 1962 C.E.;
has turned away, supremely indifferent
to my little grief ; or can't hear as well
as She once did. So this shadowy smudge
of ice, gas and dust, returning as it does
once in 10,000 years, is only another
phenomenon, like Elvis's claimed return
or the discovery of Hitler, alive
and living with Eva Braun in Argentina.
In the cold the clicking branches snap
and crackle, and snowfields give off
an unearthly glow all the way from Virgo
to constellation Perseus. The star-snow
of space, as I stand in the field looking up,
is like facing eternity alone. Alone
and speechless, as my mother was
as death carried her, high up
and away from us in a shrouded sky,
but refused either to claim her or set her down.
She must have been lonely then.
She died in the dreadful season
before Easter, and when Easter came,
there was no one. Hosannahs went up,

celebrations took place, prayers were answered
elsewhere, God's breath warmed some other
earth than this, another galaxy burst open,
and the seraphim stars whose light cut clear through here
into the frosted earth, saw my little stick-figure
standing in a snowfield, and the billions of other
stick-figures, winked at each other
knowingly, and continued to look on.

Ron Overton

Two Stories

After the exhilaration of jazz at Sweet Basil
I'm walking instead of a taxi, feeling good,
letting the quiet close back in.
Passing Madison Square, one-time home of the insolvent arm
of the Statue of Liberty, I see the dark shapes
on every bench–boxes, blankets, a heaped coat....
It doesn't look too bad, a kind of night harbor,
canvas covering the sleeping hulls. A limo speeds by,
rattling the obligatory manhole cover, and a shadow rises up,
then falls back into what I assume is a reasonable sleep.
It's two o'clock, the air is August mild, the portals
of the Flatiron Building glow like a spaceship.
I feel safe and a little foolish, alone,
walking past this secret society. Who am I
to feel sorry, to write a poem with a bullet between my teeth?
There is a sweetness in the air, a swirling sense of time
standing still, a mystery–like a father watching
his children sleep, their sorrow ahead of them, but happy now
in their timeless circle of dreams.

But there is also the winter.
And that is another story.

Robert Parham

Swan Song for Deconstruction

How curious ever to have celebrated the undoing
while ignoring the undone, determined what has not
been said, instead of how to say it, considered

as valuable those words which vaporized their betters,
the way such flaxen probabilities dissolve, for some,
what others know, quite critically, is still poetry.

Let me sing this song for Derrida and Paul de Man
then, and others in that tinny chorus, a tune
for bedlam's choir and less than minor poets:
music can be made, is more than simply in beholding,
and while a swan song is, you know, perhaps no song at all,
it is, for some like me, a kind of music to the ear.

Linda Pastan

The News of the World

Like weather, the news
is always changing and always
the same. On a map
of intractable borders
armies ebb and flow.
In Iowa a roof is lifted
from its house like a top hat

caught in a swirl of wind.
Quadruplets in Akron.
In Vilnius a radish
weighing 50 pounds.
And somewhere
another city falls
to its knees.

See how the newsprint
comes off on our once
immaculate hands
as we wrap the orange peel
in the sports page
or fold into the comics
a dead bird

the children found
and will bury
as if it were the single
sparrow whose fall
God once promised
to note, if only
on the last page.

Near the End of the Century

Stained with beauty and the deep
arterial color of loss, October
calls us out into the cooling air,
into the diaspora of leaves,
whole tribes scattered–poplar
and elm, between tree

and smoke. And we stand
wrapping our frail arms
around our bodies, as the golden
light tarnishes before our eyes,
and we remember all
we had thought to forget.

Molly Peacock

Goodbye Hello in the East Village

Three tables down from Allen Ginsberg we sit
in JJ's Russian Restaurant. My old friend,
who's struggled for happiness, insists
on knowing why I'm happy. An end
to my troubles of the century? *"Listen Molly, if I
didn't know you so well, I'd think you were
faking this good cheer,"* she says, her eyes
bright openings like a husky's eyes in its fur.
(My friend is half an orphan. It's cold in here.)
The East Village shuffles past JJ's window,
and we hear Allen order loudly in the ear
of the waitress, *"Steamed only! No cholesterol!"*
"I could tell you it's my marriage, Nita,
and how much I love my new life in two countries,
but the real reason," I beam irresistibly at a
dog walker with 8 dogs on leashes in the freezing
evening outside JJ's window where we sit,
"is that I'm *an orphan*. It's *over*. They're
both dead." Her lids narrow her eyes to a slit
of half-recognition. "I couldn't say this,"–there!
The waitress plunks two bowls of brilliant magenta
borscht, pierogi, and hunks of challah
–"to just *anybody*,"–jewel heaps of food on Formica

–only to you, who wouldn't censure me,
since you've witnessed me actually fantasize
chopping their heads from their necks from their limbs
to make a soup of the now dead Them to feed
the newly happily alive Me.

                        An old order is dimmed,
just as now the U.S., its old enemy
the USSR vaporized, disarmed itself,
nearly wondering what a century's fuss
was all about . . . what *was* my fuss about? (The wealth
of relief after decades of distrust,
makes you wonder why you did it, until
you remind yourself of how it was.)
But even a struggle to the death is leveled
in the afterlife of relief. A bevel
in the glass of America has connected
along a strip of this life to the window
of JJ's restaurant connecting Nita and me, wed
to the nightlife on Second Avenue, though
in reflection only, the reflection that now perfectly
joins Ginsberg with his steamed vegetables
and us with our steamy borscht and pierogi
to the ice-pocked sidewalk, God's table,
full of passersby, pointing occasionally to Allen,
joined now by an Asian boy, but more often
just hurrying past in the cold as we eat
the food of a previous enemy
and find it brightly delicious–*it is meet
and right so to do*–in the world now ours,
the century's hours hurtling behind
like snow-wake off an empty dogsled.
Old friends, we rest, not talking, well fed,
since at this cold dark moment things are fine.

Edmund Pennant

Mahane Yehuda
Outdoor Market, Jerusalem

Palming a melon
the woman sounds it
with the heel of her hand,
listening for sweet densities.

She is a solemn type
and takes her time.

When God looked over
the newly made world,
He, too, took His time
and decided it was good.

She shoulders the crowd towards
the man she must bargain with,

remembering how God backed down
in the face of Abraham's plea
not to destroy Sodom for the sake
of fifty righteous, forty, thirty,
twenty, ten... she smiles.

*At that moment the suicide bomber
pressed the toggle on his belt.*

Stuart Peterfreund

Yom Hashoa: The Reading of the Names
Northeastern University, 27 April 1995

1.
From the salt wastes of alphabet, the wilderness
where they will always seek to enter into rest,
we call the burnt back from the furnace to witness
Our *yizkor*, our *aliyah*, our embrace. The list
Unveils the fifty-year diaspora since they
Last cried the watchword of their faith. Here we perform
no Mozart, no Schubert. Our solo voices play
inventions so much barer than sonata form:
the surnames are the bass; those given, the melody.
We take frequent repeats for names this beautiful—
as though God savored *Cohen, Anna* and *Emily*;
Davidoff, Chaim and *Leah; Goldstein, Samuel.*
We challenge more than murder: acting in cold type,
we undo night and fog, stripe after rotten stripe.

2.
While it is light out all their names proclaim the one.
While it is light out numerals of midnight blue
melt from their arms and flee to abendland, where soon

the sun will follow. In the interim, we do
the little to be done–commend those names to that deep air,
where history dreams dreams of other universes,
and vow they will receive the best perpetual care.
Meanwhile, their souls, which spin like ashen dervishes,
go calling after the red earth, their true birthright.
No use to invoke the other cosmology:
we know the names for all that surrounds us–dark and light,
dry land and water. Our dominion?–irony.
We speak this day from night; we speak this land from sea:
though we speak out all their names, we can let none be.

Jane Piirto

Fraternity Bar in Athens, Georgia

they were shoulder to shoulder
drinking beer and playing pool
the room stunk of smoke from hell
the light under the bar shone orange

I sat at the end
talked to who came by
of race in Georgia

inexhaustibly they spewed
heedless of Mark Fuhrman's ignominy
that word
northerners don't dare to use
and many other words prefaced
by "they" and "them"

shaved almost bald
in fashion in front-faced
corduroy baseball caps
("I'd never wear my hat backwards like them")
beside their long-haired white-toothed beauties
they assumed a tribal camaraderie
from the color of my skin

told me their scarred inner hearts
while I smoked their cigarettes
in words I didn't want to hear
in words I wish I hadn't asked

at 2 a.m. they bid me bye
"y'all come back again, Professor
when you move to town"
in a conspiracy of skin and tribe
I kept my shame.

David Ray

An Incident in Union, Carolina

Medea, it seems, returns to the stage
more and more often. It all crashed
down on her, she said. Her life
had skittered out of control.

What else could one do,
with both husband and lover grown harsh,
but strap the children into the car
and watch it roll into the river.

And once on stage, what could one do
but plead with the kidnappers,
fictive and black as the men
she was taught to fear? Forty years back,

perhaps less, a black would have been lynched.
She begs for the return of her babes,
she tells them and the world how she loves them
and while on stage she may well feel

the euphoric release of an actress or one
who has managed to rise above facts
or to change them. It is not what she meant.
Had she not intended to take her own life?

Should they not take that into account?
Saint or great sinner, she's left the real world
behind, spun away from its moorings.
Yet after the play under the bright lights

she disappears into a jail cell.
She will melt into her weeping.
The flood bore her children away and her
with it. It is all soon a fable, a classic.

Progress Report

"The Air Force will pair man, woman for duty in underground missile silos." –News Item

For the first time, the Air Force
plans to assign a man and a woman
together, deep underground.

What a transition, it seems,
from the first couple at Eden,
having come to this, babysitting

a monster that may become
murderous at any moment.
Asked what they do, they say

mostly play cards or chess.
(At least they're smart enough
to play chess, not just checkers—

there's hope in that.) But smart
enough to think twice before
launching? Not at all. The rules

are clear, and forbid a pacifist
impulse. But what if they give
in to temptation, are making love

when the order comes honking–
if they run naked and panicked
but cannot find their keys? Both

must, after all, stick in a key–
equal shares in the sin of it.
Last time, Eve alone took the blame.

But it's wishful thinking I know,
for the venial, personal sin
to overcome the one

that will kill without regard
to who or what is on target.
The requisite numbness

is in place, and all the humanity
has been trained out of them.
They will not be making love.

Wrappings

It was a sea of plastic, cellophane,
vinyl—those thousands of bouquets
tossed on Princess Di's coffin.

But maybe nobody noticed
an absence of the scent
of roses, gardenias, and baby's breath.

Colors were muted, lost under
those icy surfaces glimmering.
Red may have been too stark,

white too pure, blue too much
like the bride's garter to allow
it all to be displayed to the sky,

to the mobs who gawked and craned,
shoved to get close and yet did not
wish to behold red as stark as blood,

as the damascene rose. They came
for plastic and vinyl, cellophane,
and with hope that the coffin might

              turn out to be glass.

Judy Ray

Scheherazade
for Salman Rushdie, 14 February

Anonymous, we send our valentines
to your place of no name.
Is it raining there? How many masks
must the child of midnight claim?

Your sharp wit cut the world
with hyperbole and diabolic satire.
"Shame!" cries Islam,
calling assassins for hire.

"Shame!" echoes back, but we glance around
with almost imperceptible furtive shuffle,
thinking of threats, of firebombs,
of translators abruptly muffled.

We wear masks in the act of writing.
But we should be free
to choose our masks
as we choose our words, carefully.

We gather up and read the banned, burned words.
We think of you and of others exiled, jailed.
Is it raining there? This red-edged banner
bears the letters of your name, nailed

to the wall on this Valentine's raining noon.
More than a thousand and one nights
have passed. May you spin
your tales on into the light.

James Reiss

Skimming Toward Blue
Elegy for a Poet

1.
So what if he drank, fucked like a skunk
& stomped on his colleagues also drunk.

He was no vegetarian saint, by God.
No avuncular hubby, he did what he did

because he was smitten by poetry &
a passion for paradise which he designed

by writing & wilding–to hell with the tea
cups & rose hips in drawing rooms. He

was at home on a river bank playing guitar
or in bed with the chairman's wife while her

ponytail played with a line in his head.
No child-murdering creep, he did what he did

because he was still the invincible kid
barnstorming & hellraising until he was dead.

2.
If in life he sometimes made good on his word,
kept promises & was faithful in fact

words were what he was best at, finally:
his descriptions of fog not evasions

but a clear lens, a declaration of dependence
on meadows, wet pebbles, & sheep

in the rain rightly rendered, plainspoken
in patters & plinks. Oh he was good

at making myths out of molehills, tunneling
under the truth to uncover a Truth

that belied his deception, his greed for humongous
distortions, & lit up a landscape completely

appointed with moss-mazy rivers
which rippled with riddles yet wound their way home.

3.
On the way home in DC the night he clambered
out of my car & planted himself by the gas pumps

he looked like a line backer for the Redskins.
Who calls him a shark in the end zone?

Evenings in Leesburg he fondled the mike
with delight while he rattled off facts,

I thought of him as Commander in Chief.
Who calls him a pig in a war room

of pleasure? Yeah, he spoke about women
in droves. Yeah, he clicked off my tape recorder

& whispered no wilderness glinting with rivers,
no fifth of Glenlivit at the end of the day

could compare with a girl in a black negligee
or an underage boy in a swimsuit.

4.
But listen up, friends, if he called himself a fiend
& a monster, in my book he

is a troubadour who will lure us
to hear him again when the tuneless

fin-de-siècle scribblers leave the room.
Soon his split lines crackling like firewood

his anapests' luminous stresses
will light up a landscape where foxes

will lie down with hounds while we stand
up in the millennium, bent on reclaiming

his riverine music, recalling
torrential undercurrents of feeling

he brought to the surface, his silver canoe
abob on white water Christ! skimming toward blue.

Pattiann Rogers

The Kingdom of Heaven

      inside of which careen
the wrecked suns of obliterating
stellar furies and smelting quasars
ejecting the seething matter of stars
in piercing shocks wrenching and spewing
blasted flares and ash of incinerated
planets whose roaring eruptions
and scorching thunders, in the slightest
proximity, would boil and melt the ear
to spent char long before those sounds
could ever reach the ear as sound.
      inside of which exist
the serenities of this fading summer
evening, the motion of wind in slow,
shifting passions down from redcedar
and netleaf, across the easy flight
of creeks and bluegrasses, within
the peace of possibilities created
by a single cricket in his place,
the assurance of blindnesses behind
my eyes closed on this hillside,
earth pressing against my body
      inside of which wheel
fine solar particles and microscopic

constellations issuing and collapsing,
waging transformations, gatherings
and dissolutions through bones and veins,
circling and spinning in pursuits and purposes
with bloody powers and strategies
      inside of which is one
deity proven by the faith of sleep
and the imagination to exist throughout
these realms of such measured light
and destruction

William Pitt Root

Writing Late Through the Night of the Tiananmen Square Massacre

1. *Language That Follows War Like Hyenas*
I'm thinking of Tiananmen Square, of how awkward
Chinese can be on an English tongue, of the tanks,
warhorses of our age, bearing down on the brave who
stood their ground too long, who died under the treads,

their bodies, according to witnesses, popping like melons.
I'm thinking of the language that follows war like hyenas,
disposing of the dead, the mad cackling in the dark
as the powerful jaws of distortion do their work.

Because brothers, sisters, sons, daughters are translated
into "hooligans" for dreaming, as only the innocent can,
of justice without war, and for speaking truth to power,
hundreds at the hands of thousands are dying tonight.

2. *Strange Music*
And I'm thinking of the strange music of war:
The skittering clatter of irontracks on stone pavement,
ponderous, monstrous, with an awkward crab-like agility,
and the howitzer's whoosh and boom, the high shells

soundlessly arcing overhead whistling just before
it's all over for those who hear but cannot run
far enough to avoid the firestorm and shrapnel.
And I'm thinking, almost with nostalgia,

of a time I never knew, when Roman horsemen could ride

certain of victory over any foot soldiers, all of them
now dust, the last breath of each so long mingled
with our air that every breath we take includes

molecules of theirs. The horsemen rode mounts trained
to dance to the strains of particular songs, lifting
their forelegs in chorus, prancing to this side,
then that, pride of the Roman legions they were,

anathema to their enemies. Except that these heathens
had heard of the dancing horses so often they spoke
of them by their campfires, sometimes to praise,
sometimes to curse, sometimes to joke about them,

relieving their fears with "what-if's." Until one such
what-if did happen. As always, the Romans approached
riding in formation, shields raised, swords drawn,
approached at a trot–the better to chase down

hapless fools fleeing before them at their own pace,
lopping off heads from above and behind. When the ranks
parted before them, as always, like reeds in the wind,
how strange must have been the first startling sight

as bedraggled musicians began rising up before them,
lifting their horns and cymbals, rasping at strings,
beating on drums, catching just enough of that melody
configured in the warhorses' hearts to divide them

from the plans of their riders, to start them prancing
and keep them sidestepping while their startled riders
cried out commands the music countermanded. Disarray,
disarray–no longer a unified front, no longer the

shod lockstep propelling the wall of brazen shields on.
Gone the solar certainty blazing from visored eyes. Disarray!
Disarray! On boomed the drums, crudely makeshift; on
piped the flutes, frail against spears; on rang the singing

horns raised to the sky; and on danced the dancers
in brilliant regalia–as foot soldiers ran among them,
thrusting up spears, long swords, jabbing, hacking;
and then came the archers running up from behind:

thrum of the bowstrings echoing, echoing,

clanging of arrows on helmets, ringing of sword against
shield and bone as the horsemen lurched and the horsemen
pitched and the horses under them danced as they fell.

3. *Mist Swirling Skyward*
I write thinking of you, my distant brothers and sisters:
I write even as soldiers of the 27th Army drag your bodies
—bodies they deny—to mass cremation. Bonfires, bone fires
consuming your hopes and banners in a single flame

peeling the flesh back like parchment from your hearts,
smoke so heavy, so richly laden, mounting the Forbidden City....
How can leaders continue to lie, when our own stars
beam down the readable imagery of slaughter?

How can they not remember how far, how long, the honest
innocence of ashes drift? Yes, I'm writing through the night—
how else not be helpless, not be maddened as this human dream
yet again is massacred? Now I'm hearing of spring rain

that washes your blood-gleam from those pavingstones
politicians insisted your living presence "defiled";
I hear how dawn sun draws that spring shower up out of stones
in skeins of mist swirling skyward ghostly as snow geese.

4. *A World Free to Change Channels*
You, whose names once were strange as copper on my tongue,
sisters of the spirit song, brothers of the broken bone,
how, ever again, can there be strangeness between us
now we've seen you bleeding freedom's common price?

And yet, one knows it will be so. Already tonight,
angry fans of the telecast Oakland Raiders' game
are calling in, in droves, bitterly complaining
that their show has been pre-empted by your martyrdom.

Now we witness students, teachers, day-laborers, dreamers
signing "Freedom" to a world free to change channels,
raising an outcry so contagious that plain folks bearing
straw baskets of fishes and bread, fruits and flowers,

suddenly straighten backs bent by lifetimes of submission
to those moving only to the tunes of their own courts,
those bowing only to one another, those who suck the juices,
spit out human rinds. Workers upright in the streets stood

before the first soldiers, petition their mercy for you
as you pled Justice and Freedom for all. In this country,
such blood-born terms–richly abused, freely translated into
tongues of shameless greed and glib deceit–occasionally

gag us. Like apples publicly polished, privately poisoned. Yet
some fruits, first savored, may so transform inspired tongues
that they can sing the old songs new–as when
the long downtrodden conspire with young dreamers, as when

the defenseless stand, arms akimbo, before trucks cunningly wedged
to block a tank's passage. As when the young daring
to speak truth to old Father power, see power hesitate,
listening to its own old song played back in your new key.

<u>Eugene Ruggles</u>

Somalia Kneeling

There are millions of holes
with arms and legs
walking through Somalia.
For seven years they have been
listening for water, her descendants.
They are opening wider everyday
as they swallow the heat.
The sun never stops blowing though them,
as though they were disciples.
Their only shade falls
from the lungs of Ethiopia and Sudan.
The holes burn deeper
between the arms and legs of Somalia.
The younger ones drink
from the emptiness at the bottom,
they slide from the arms holding them
and the emptiness follows them.
They sink without tears,
even for death there is no water.
Their blood will no longer
make its pilgrimage toward the heart
to eat. The sand is their sanctuary. At night,
another famine rages around the living,

as young packs of automatic weapons crawl
and steal closer to their flanks to feed.
The millions of holes are beginning to kneel
With a great silence, their knees
are as black tongues entering the sand.
There is no bush that will burn
for them in their desert. They are the bush.
A grain of rice could cover their sleep.
They curl around their holes
waiting to be filled
with a crust of the world's seed.
As they reach for the map
made of sackcloth laid out before them,
they are filled with the flies
and the ashes of sand.
Insects anoint their eyelids.
We have come this far
from the cave.

February Eleventh Nineteen Ninety-Nelson Mandela Walks Into Freedom
"For out of prison he cometh to lead..." –Ecclesiastes 4:14

He arrives
with twenty seven scars
of light in his spine,
his keepers coil their whips
around handles of ivory as the chains
surrounding Johannesburg begin to rust.
From Cape Town to Soweto and north
his family begins to inhale his breath,
to gaze upward through his eyes
and to move to the great hymn
of his heart. It is the day
when the prisoners free the guards,
when lava pours from the sea,
when the streams open their lungs
to breathe, and it is the day
when the hills of dead young African men
begin to stir in the bones of their mothers.

Grace Schulman

Prayer
for Agha Shahid Ali

Yom Kippur: wearing a bride's dress bought in Jerusalem,
I peer through swamp reeds, my thought in Jerusalem.

Velvet on grass. Odd, but I learned young to keep this day
just as I can, if not as I ought, in Jerusalem.

Like sleep or love, prayer may surprise the woman
who laughs by a stream, or the child distraught in Jerusalem.

My Arab dress has blue-green-yellow threads
the shades of mosaics hand-wrought in Jerusalem.

Jews, Muslims, prize, like the blue-yellow Dome of the Rock;
like strung beads-and-cloves said to ward off the drought in Jerusalem.

Both savor things that grow wild–coreopsis in April,
the rose that buds late, like an afterthought, in Jerusalem.

While car-bombs flared, an Arab poet translated
Hebrew verses whose flame caught in Jerusalem.

And you, Shahid, sail Judah Halevi's sea as I,
on Ghalib's, course like an Argonaut in Jerusalem.

Stone lions pace the Sultan's gate while almonds bloom
into images, Hebrew and Arabic, wrought in Jerusalem.

No words, no metaphors, for knives that gore flesh
on streets where the people have fought in Jerusalem.

As this spider weaves a web in silence,
may Hebrew and Arabic be woven taut in Jerusalem.

Here at the bay, I see my face in the shallows
and plumb for the true self our Abraham sought in Jerusalem.

Open the gates to rainbow-colored words
of outlanders, their sounds untaught in Jerusalem.

My name is Grace, Chana in Hebrew–and in Arabic.
May its meaning, "God's love," at last be taught in Jerusalem.

The Wedding

Late spring in Caesaria, Herod's harbor,
now a city of Roman ruins, quiet
but for gull cries in the whitehot light
of midday. People gather at the shore

as if to see a sword dance, to hear drums
and dagger-beats on shields–the pre-biblical
rites of this region–not the nuptials
of military lovers: agile, slim

army border-guards on active duty
wearing pearl-white wedding costumes, she,
satin and lace, he, linen, stiffly
pressed. Seeming too young to fight *or* marry,

they pose for photographs, the sea exploding
on rocks, and, shoes cast off, run on hot sand
to the marriage canopy, a covering
to cast off demons. It snaps in high wind,

their sacred roof, a dazzling cotton
embroidered prayer-shawl whose supporting poles
are rifles held by three men and a woman
in combat fatigues. There, before them all,

a rabbi intones the seven benedictions,
offers wine, hears vows and blesses them,
and blesses children who sing psalms. At sundown,
when the bridal pair change into uniforms,

a shot rings out. A woman screams and falls.
Three of the groom's attendants grab the rifles
that held the canopy, fall to the ground
at the stammer of guns, rub faces with wet sand,

and, shouldering their weapons, run to the sea
firing at men who creep out of a dinghy
that's dragged aground. One of the intruders,
his buoyant gait so like the bride's

that he seems an invited cousin, drops to the shore,
face down. Another stranger staggers

a few yards, bleeding, his stubby fingers
frozen on his gun. Bodies pitch forward,

arms and legs flail. Silence. White garments strewn
like a book's blown pages, the groom bends down
to lift the prayer-shawl that lies, torn,
mud-splattered. He folds it, kisses it, then

flings his red beret to the darkening
sand. Leading his bride to a small car,
he turns back for a time, as though to hear,
through mounting wave-sounds, what the children sang.

Ruth L. Schwartz

The City
in memory of Ariel Jimenez
*That was my dream. Just to walk down the street,
holding hands with another man.–Andy*

Saint Francis in his brown robe in the garden honors
every butterfly and bird, every living thing,
and in the city named for him,
where *gay* is a spoken language,
even the trim on the gingerbread houses
dances with color, up and down the hills
to the ocean, the very edge of the world we know.
And it is not the city itself which is killing the pretty men,
though because they came here from anywhere else,
Mexico, Colombia, Grenada, Puerto Rico,
Cleveland, Milwaukee, Nashville, desperation,
all lured by the echo of open kisses,
because they came here with blood and bodies unpoisoned,
and will fall here, most of them,
straitjacketed by IV tubes,
oxygen nosepieces, stainless steel bed walls,
it is hard not to think,
*if they had not come here,
they would have survived.*
I am driving one of them to the hospital
and still the others stride toward us, against the light,
their butterfly faces, their perfect apple asses,
their hands in each others' hands, while the oldies

station plays Dylan knock-knock-knocking on heaven's door.
We all came here from somewhere else,
but because we know this city,
because we chose it like a lover, winding our lives
through its streets as if caressing them,
we imagine the city knows us,
recognizes us
in its invisible heart,
even as death pats its hands
around the sand of our bodies
as if sculpting us, and we open
our mouths to the tide.

Myra Shapiro

Columbus Circle

Looking at the moon next to World Trade, reading *moon*
     for *noon* in a Holman poem,
I marvel at those *o's* circling everywhere my eyes fasten:
     breasts, galactic boulders
I climbed in Bronx Park to amount to something.
     They stood
like station stops the train pulls into. Without them
     I would scatter. That's what
Columbus gave to this millennium: a round world.
     But soon it's 2001
and a fellow wrote at the end of a poem:
     Get around round.
He means there's outer space, there's no going back
     to the place you started,
homeless in mid-air, no one to care, musical chairs
     where the chair's not there,
freefall. Yet I don't let go, I hold to the soul
     of a New York girl-
hood, pooh-poohing the strip, turning tail on the mall.

John Sherman

Cages

in memphis tennessee
tuesdays at the zoo
were reserved for blacks

which is another way of saying:
sundays mondays wednesdays thursdays fridays and saturdays
were not

on tuesdays only:
the giraffes came onto the grass
and let the boys and girls
slide down their necks

on tuesdays at the zoo in memphis tennessee
peacocks brought forth six gorgeous feathers
hidden in their tails for six days

on tuesdays:
flamingos lifted both feet
in the air
and remained aloft

on tuesdays in memphis tennessee even the snakes behaved

my future wife chose a wildebeest
who put golden flowers in her hair
then whispered to her of serengeti

she placed her red shoes on his hind feet
and they danced

laughing
laughing

finally:
suddenly:
at five o'clock
little girls cried
and hugged the bears goodbye

cats licked boys faces
and rubbed their purring chins
against nappy heads

the white guards awoke

and cage doors rang shut

Enid Shomer

Writing a Formal Poem the Winter After Your Death
in memoriam Judson Jerome

Today the sky spun wire-thin strands
of sunlight as if to bale the snowdrifts like July
wheat. Last summer, a pump delivering
morphine through your neck, you taught formal
poems and read your latest work, your white
pompadour like a baton that stressed the time

of every verse. Meanwhile, on some clock the time
of your life ticked down to twenty-one stranded
days. Your head on the pillow, white on white,
you dictated bursts dazzling as July's
fireworks: a reply from the Dark Lady using the form
of the Bard, a memoir about communal life

and the ménage à trois that outlived
most marriages, a poem about timing
one's death for *Modem Maturity*. Depression was a form
utterly foreign to you. *Luck*, you claimed, *a strand
of happy DNA*. Two Julys
ago I watched you cast off frothy white

chains as you swam half a mile, white
corpuscles cleansing your blood, your liver
still good. The spring tides this July,
blue hooks of the moon, retracted the sea for a time.
In place of the water where you swam, the strand
lay broadened for miles, crab holes deforming

it like metastases beneath the skin. Formal
poems, you said, like sonnets, yield sweeter wit
and moral certitude. Rhymes are invisible strands
that connect the impossible, the way a pump delivers

the sky gushing from the land, its lever marking time
like a clock hand stuck on the moment in July

when I realized you'd been taken in the July
of your life. At first, you didn't reform
your daily routine, refusing death's sway before its time.
Then dementia did the final edit. While morphine whited
out the pain, you spewed venom on your life,
denied you ever loved your spouse, the child stranded

at the mental age of six. Now time serves up a posthumous
book wearing white hair, a stranded smile. July
revised the formal message in each cell from *live* to *die*.

Jeffrey Skinner

Late Afternoon, Late in the Twentieth Century

Dusk in Creason's Park comes on slow,
darkening the folds in the children's jackets,
the fall air beer-colored, thick
as remembrance, and the climbed trees shiver
down last leaves. I try to watch both kids
at once, though they tend to drift
from one steel-and-colored-plastic
jerryrig of slides, bridges, and swings,
to another, independent, drawn to separate
peers, and I have to call them back
into one field of vision. There are other
parents here, sitting on the sawhorse
picnic benches, talking or smoking, their
arms spread the table's length, their legs
straight out. One man in his fifties
sits alone, an open briefcase before him,
making notes on a legal pad; office
alfresco... It is close to finished,
this century. Soon the 1 will change
to a simple 2, like a circuit changing
its mind from yes to no, like the short
step of a wounded soldier. We have filled
the universe with blood again, to no
one's surprise. And by the river's edge

we complained of thirst, we eyed
the forests and filled them with glare.
We said this edge will fit that space
and it did–the concrete oozed through
wooden forms, a thousand blank faces
rose above us, and we were happy
as a smooth surface, as a just-shot
arrow. We ridiculed the old questions,
stabbing our fingers in their leather chests
until they'd had enough, and headed back
to the salt caverns. We found love shivering
in a bus station and took her home,
tenderly sponging off the superficial
wounds. We gave her tea before the fire.
When she grew old we sold the company
and put her back on the bus. We died,
and the others were outraged, they pounded
fists, they petitioned, they did everything
but join us. Then they joined us. We
starved language, until the bones showed
through and the head dropped off
and rolled away, laughing like an idiot....
The dusk in Creason's Park comes on, slowly,
and the parents reel their children in
on the soft hook of their names, and they all
drift toward their cars and thoughts
of food and sleep. *Girls*, I yell, *let's
go!* and they come breathless and glazed
from play. In them I am well pleased,
and would build a city for their future.
But I will not take credit for their failures.
Lord, they are close to me as my skin
and I snarl when the dress is torn, when
the milk spills. Hear me. I am still that lost.

Elizabeth Spires

1999

In a hundred years, we won't be here,
replaced by the unimaginable, a flash,
a whir, as forests fall, rise up again,
and houses that we lived in disappear.
Changing our form, will we come back then?
Or stay underground, quiet and companionable?

Will poems be written then?
Whose hand will write them?
Will someone stand, time's ghost,
as I do now, in a peeling gazebo with antique
posts and scroll work, here on the edge
of a lake, the edge of time so close?

To the west, the mountains are immovable,
a sheer cliff face that no one can climb.
Shadows play on the lake's surface
as clouds race by, seeded and shining,
a wind from the north whipping the water
into waves, unreadable to the eye.

In a hundred years, will the mountains
exhaust themselves? Will the lake move on?
Will my hand, severed from mind, lie fallow
forever? For a week or two, summer is endless.
Then we fall back into lives that rush forward
with terrible speed, our future glimpsed in dreams:

the gazebo gone, the dusty road paved over,
its blind curves straightened out, leading
nowhere we want to go, the sun and moon
whirling brightly above the figure of a tree,
its branches black as char, where no bird
sings and no wind blows through ever.

Once, all flesh and shadow, we prayed
for our own permanence. Now we stand
in the center of a vacancy that is the center
of the new, asking what will be left
when each thing goes. Our answer an echo–
The singing. Only the singing.

Julie Suk

Leaving the World We've Loved Speechless

The letter A is a tent that held us for a while.
Now we're restless to leave the alphabet
and ride off into numbers.

But numbers can't divine
the luminous grove we could happen upon,
you and I stretched on the same sliver of time,
its stream winding down into fragrance,
our shadows now plaited, now loose.

In the warm intersection of sex and love,
the mouth puckers as soon as we're born,
starved no matter how often and deep
we push into someone else.

Numbers tell how many fall out, but fail
to fathom a woman's grief
tossing on a bed she can't fill.

The purity of numbers deceives us
into thinking they're true,
could never be found in a stranger's arms,

but numbers are wasted on wars
that continue to rough up the contours of history,
the landscape defined by a blast of white,
the grass we greened, gone, the mare
no longer nuzzling the child's palm.

Maybe *Voyager*, floating in its frigid sea of stars,
will land and voices once more disembark.
Absurd to think our slow-motion scatter of dust
is the beginning and end of words–
those lights announcing we've come, we've gone.

William Sylvester

Political Horn Book

What a preacher "Red Hot" Chillingworth was
Until brought down by Hester, tea, or stamps
Meet him in the street, he made good sense
Pastor says, "I never read anything they care to stamp"
He'd say: "Everyone knows we all need tea"
Sun goes down, darkness comes,
Tea sorts the pains around a bit
Between the aches of sitting down and getting up
Weeding, pulling, pushing, stooping pains
Warming tea a mothering care from the mother land
Shopkeepers figured otherwise
Tea dropped into the water
Sent the price into the sky
Pastor says we all get grace if we do good works
Good works alone won't get us grace
I never knew which way he meant
Both may be right for all I know
Good works don't go far for hunger, though
I think of the tea we used to have
Before sickness took them all
Buried them one by one, left alone
For my sins, whatever they were

Merchants set up coffee houses for the Harvard crowd
Ships and trade, harvests good for some, lots of money
Nobody minds the cost of coffee or thinks of tea

She was no tea drinker, standing up in church
Big bosom'd, broad hipped woman, fearsome sight
Called him hypocrite, horrible man, she claimed
He abused her four times three years
She made me hear the bumping bed, rustling sheets
I stared at her, but every one else looked at him
Hating him, too, a growl about to start until
A little old lady walked down the aisle
Straight up to the pulpit and turned around
Mrs Chillingworth
She settled it right then, or so I thought

"Never happened" and everyone was quiet
"And if it did" she turned to Hester
"I'd cast the first stone
Bible says I've got the right; I'd
Keep on casting until she died"
She's won, I thought, they'd kill Hester
Sooner than the Pastor, but Mrs C made
Her big mistake, making it so personal
"You are loyal to nobody at all"
You could hear the hatred sparkle up
Growing, about to break out like some huge wave
Sinking a ship to the bottom, they stared
At the Pastor and his wife, beginning to curse
to cuss right in Church and then I knew
They didn't say it but the truth flashed out

The Chillingworths are LOYALISTS
(international, un-American pacifists)
They ran out of the Church but couldn't escape
Hearing that Chillingworths were soft on
Indentured servants, runaway apprentices and
Talked to red faced unbaptized heathens
Little boys piped in falsetto:
"Everyone knows we all need tea" or sing-song
"I never read anything they stamp"
Hester wore a letter A for Abuse
Walked up and down in front of the Church
Or followed them singing an old, old tune
"I saw an A in the sky with diamonds"
Or chanted in a way I didn't fully hear
"Taxation mumblmumble tyranny"

All the others got what they wanted it seems
Stopped the taxes, merchants got the profit:
The Chillingworths escaped to Maryland or Canada
Hester became a preacher, accused of heresy
She kept on traveling south until she wasn't noticed
I sold my land, paid off my debts, mostly
Got this job in a Coffee house serving drinks
I can't afford to buy, Stranger, that's all
The news I know now you tell me
Who is this Thomas Jefferson? And... and...
...what's her name?

Susan Terris

Boxcar at the Holocaust Museum

Assaulted by brick and steel, my sister and I cross
the glass bridge between then and now, touch
Szumsk, the Polish town
our grandparents came from, walk into
Ejszyszki Tower eyeing photo doppelgängers
of relatives we call the monkey aunts,
of an uncle who couldn't skate the '36 Olympics,
of our parents, ourselves.

My younger sister has married a Baptist, raised
children who don't believe they are Jews;
yet she–riveted–is moving snail's-pace.
So when I come upon it, I am alone.
It's an old red cattle car like those from
our Missouri childhood, counted as they
clacked by full of livestock
due for slaughter. But this one is different.
To avoid passing through, I pretend
to examine oxidized razors, forks,
tea strainers, then metal instruments
of torture which up close
become umbrella frames. I check my watch,
consider flight...

                yet as I turn, I see my sister
by the boxcar unwilling to enter. *Why are
we here?* Hurrying toward her, I move past
cart, suitcases, hat boxes. *What will it tell us?*
For a moment, we are side by side, aware of
primal, physical comfort. Then together
we step in. It is dark. We do not
speak. After 50 years, stench still saturates
the boards. As I inhale it, I feel fingers
tug at the pleats of my skirt,
at my sweater, my hands. Sweaty heads
I can't see butt me, begging for refuge,
those who would not have been spared:
my children, my sister's Mischling children,
my own Mischling grandchildren.

Suddenly, a soprano voice echoes around us.
Choo-choo. Turning, we see a boy-child
havened between parents.
He smiles, nods sweetly, beckoning to us and to
the invisible hordes pressed close. *Choo-choo,*
he repeats. *Choo-choo. All aboard...*

Nadja Tesich

My Eyes and His
for my brother Steve Tesich

Be my eyes, he asked in a dream.
In Serbian it was, very unusual for him.
And in Serbian I said *hoću,*
I promise I will.
And the same night I see:
a homeless man old gray
sleeps hugging himself
on cement
on Broadway, 102nd Street,
a child junkie prostitute
screams and throws a Coke bottle
which shatters like a bomb
on cement on 102nd street.
A crowd of homeless cheers.
A shattered Coke–a substitute.
Huge well-fed cops in a blue car
gaze at us with dead liquid eyes
then move on.
From a garbage can a rat
runs over old dirty New York Times
over Dole and Clinton, Hillary and what's-her name,
over pictures, their grins all teeth,
over Bomb Iraq maybe in one corner
(was it Bomb Belgrade a year or two ago?)
I am watching for me and him.
The dead have it easy.

Hilary Tham

A True Story

A man loves a woman who hates
the way he loves her. Each time she threatens
to leave, he rapes her, masters her body
and proves his love to his satisfaction.

He's paid the price for passion many
times in a hospital bed: once, she sliced
his face open with the carving knife,
once, she broke his head with an iron skillet.
This time, she cuts off his manhood
as he sleeps the sleep of the just
spent. She flees out the door
as he screams awake with pain and loss.
Driving to freedom, she sees
the bloody thing in her hand,
flings it with horror out the window and
goes to the police station to confess.

The man is rushed to the hospital. The lost
article is located, packed in dry ice and
doctors sew skin and nerves back together.
They declare the operation a success,
dismiss the warning of the police who
delivered their find in a Coleman's cooler:
"We cannot guarantee this is the right penis,
but it is the only one we found."

The police know there are more
pricks on our streets.

Phyllis Thompson

Beauty
in memory: Linda Daniels

Was there anything in his impulsive gift of chrysanthemums
To celebrate? To make you put out your hand
Lightly, and lightly kiss your sweetheart, calling,
"Goodbye, back soon with a treat for supper," inattentive,
And leave him in a rush of late Sunday sunlight?

Choice in the supermarket—salmon and rice.
Necessity in the Cash Only checkout line.
And the fearful chance of something beautiful
That shivers for a moment in the lot before heading home,
Marked and followed, balanced in the mercy of time.

The reddening sun danced moderately on the driveway
As three medieval thugs shambled from the dusk
When you got back. Approaching your car by bloodlight,
They wrested you from it, grabbed and rubbed your body
In the drugged drift of their grotesque saraband.

Among spilled groceries, a broken ivory fan.
Beauty, there's nothing human could force you to arch
And caper, caught in a coil of albino prowlers.
What were their twisted faces like? and their words,
As they writhed in a clandestine death-revel—yours, yours.

Beauty-gone-down, Hell slides beneath a motel
On Central Avenue. But here, no change
Since you were laid among weeds under a culvert
Dead, shot once and frozen to the ground.
There's murder on the front lawn and it doesn't matter.

We're not Greeks. We can't say Hades has taken you,
All nature grieves. We don't know how to mourn
Or honor Beauty ravaged by slavering thieves
Handling their spoil. We can't make any sense of it
On your behalf. There's blood guilt, and nobody gets paid.

Things we believed in, anemic stupidity mocks
With knife or pistol. Our clamour for justice is edged
With rage, with grief, for a child's good world corrupted.
Too old to be ignorant any more, we know
The sweetest body defiled under filthy legs.

The loneliness of your last agony, bereft
Utterly among strange men! Had you lived after,
Who could have rocked you to comfort? Immortality
Gathers about you now, out of our yearning
Toward every lost ideal. But for your death, no answer.

William Trowbridge

His Greatest Moments

In the 60-second spot, he's back
to dance and Rope-a-Dope and sting,
turning couplets fast as Cyrano–Clay
proclaimed Ali, flashy in Everlasts
loose and pretty, his own brass band,
who could be watching with us now,
guard dropped as the blows rain in.

Lewis Turco

The Great Ice Storm of 'Ninety-Eight

The rains have stopped, and now the woods are crystal,
The roads are silver rivers sluicing through
This January air. We hear reports
Out of the forest that tell us boles are splitting,
Branches breaking, birches and maples spitting
Showers of ice. Now and then a pistol
Cracks nearby–a power line resorts
To sparks and even flame–gold, red and blue.

It would appear a giant has stepped upon
The upper boughs of all the trees in sight.
Darkness falls as solidly as the rain
Upon the lampglow showing in silent houses
Along these country roads, but nothing rouses
Anything to action. A nearby pond
Lies dully in its hollow, hardly frozen–
If there were streetlamps its water would drink their light.

The hours drag themselves through night. At last
Life begins once more and day by day
Men commence to mend the devastation,
But slowly, slowly. It will be weeks before
Maine is tamed again. Who will restore
Our confidence in our civilizing power
After this rain of glass? The storm is past,
For now–another broods on the horizon.
Winter will linger, and its runes are gray.

Amy Uyematsu

The Ten Million Flames of Los Angeles
A New Year's Poem, 1994

I've always been afraid of death by fire,
I am eight or nine when I see the remnants of a cross
burning on the Jacobs' front lawn,
seventeen when Watts explodes in 65,
forty four when Watts blazes again in 1992.
For days the sky scatters soot and ash which cling to my skin,
the smell of burning metal everywhere. And I recall
James Baldwin's warning about the fire next time.

> *Fires keep burning in my city of the angels,*
> *from South Central to Hollywood,*
> *burn, baby, burn.*

In 93 LA's Santana winds incinerate Laguna and Malibu.
Once the firestorm begins, wind and heat regenerate
on their own, unleashing a fury so unforgiving
it must be a warning from the gods.

> *Fires keep burning in my city of the angels,*
> *how many does it take,*
> *burn, LA, burn.*

Everybody says we're all going to hell.
No home safe
from any tagger, gangster, carjacker, neighbor.
LA gets meaner by the minute
as we turn our backs
on another generation of young men,
become too used to this condition
of children killing children.
I wonder who to fear more.

> *Fires keep burning in my city of angels,*
> *but I hear someone whisper,*
> *"Mi angelita, come closer."*

Though I ready myself for the next conflagration,
I feel myself giving in to something I can't name.
I smile more at strangers, leave big tips to waitresses,
laugh when I'm stuck on the freeway, content

just listening to B.B. King's"'Why I Sing the Blues."

"Mi angelita, mi angelita."

I'm starting to believe in a flame
which tries to breathe in each of us.
I see young Chicanos fasting one more day
in a hunger strike for education,
read about gang members preaching peace in the hood,
hear Reginald Denny forgiving the men
who nearly beat him to death.
I look at people I know, as if for the first time,
sure that some are angels. I like the unlikeliness
of this unhandsome crew–the men losing their hair,
needing a shave, those with dark shining
eyes, and the gray-haired women, rage
and grace in each sturdy step.
What is this fire I feel, this fire which breathes freely
inside without burning them alive?

Fires keep burning in my city of angels,
but someone calls to me,
"Angelita, do not run from the flame."

Julia Vinograd

Peace

Peace is invisible.
When it happens we don't notice it.
We focus on the wars inside peace
to have something to see:
war with the landlord, war with families,
war with traffic jams, war with work,
war with love.
When we go looking for peace on vacations
to a beach, or the grand canyon or camping
we quarrel, lose the mosquito repellent,
even have a good time battling the elements
and bring back a sunburn like our own bloody scalp,
but that's not peace.
Soldiers spend a whole war
tying to remember peace

and never get it into focus,
and afterwards they're too tired.
The only time we can see peace
is just before a war.
When there's a "but suddenly" feeling
lurking behind the softness of a summer evening.
When the completeness of an apple
is about to be interrupted by an army.
When the warm smell of cookies
coming out of an oven
in a sunny kitchen
is so different from poison gas.
When the glass is still unbroken.
When children can shout without guns starting up.
Today I caught myself staring
at the many colors of a damp pebble
in a vacant lot
as if they could unfold and tell me everything.
I stored those ordinary colors in my head
to defend myself when the fighting starts.
      Today I noticed peace.
      It's a very bad sign.

Chocolate Waters

Anonymous

I'm walkin' down the streets of New York City
and the tears are rollin' down my face
'cause I ain't got no apartment
& I ain't got no job
& I ain't got no lover
& I ain't got much money.
I bum a cigarette from a guy on 14th Street.
He tells me that his name is Derrick.
He's a jazz musician–out of work.
We drink from a beer can wrapped inside a paper bag
& he pisses on every other corner
& he pulls me around by the shoulders
& introduces me to
everyone as his lady

& he rips off a street guy's dope
& we get stopped by the "po-lice."
I'm walkin' down the streets of New York City
and the tears are rollin' down my face,
but I wanna give Derrick something
cause he says he's got three kids
& his mother just died
& he doesn't have the
train fare home.
So I give my last ten-dollar bill.
He palms the ten spot.
Rubs his mouth all over me.
Tries to screw me in a doorway.
I push him off, against the wall.
I have to kick him in the balls.
"Don't you know how to take a damn gift
when you get one, man?"
He thinks the only way to let me know he cares
is to put himself inside me.
I think the only way to let him know I care
is to give him money.
I slam the door into his face.
I run the four flights up to the
shelter where I'm staying for the night.
I lay down upon the mattress.
I get sick.
I get so sick I have a nightmare that I'm walkin' down the
streets of New York City
& I ain't got no apartment
& I ain't got no job
& I ain't got no lover
& I ain't got *no* money
& the tears are rollin'
                      rollin'
                                    rollin'....

Michael Waters

Miles Weeping

To hear Miles weep
   for the first time, the notes bent
      back into his spent frame to keep
   them from soaring away–
I had to click the phonograph off
   and hug myself to stop the shaking.
      I'd recognized a human cry
beyond any longing given a name.
If ever he let go that grief
   he might not touch his horn again.
      That cry rose in another country,
full-throated in awkward English.
I still have the envelope, unstamped,
   addressed to "Mother/Father," its oily
      scrap of paper torn from a primer,
the characters like the inky
root-hairs scrawling the washed-out soil.
   Lek–every boy's nickname–
      wrote he was "to be up against,"
meaning, I guess, that his future
was end-stopped, one unbroken line
   of tabletops waiting to be wiped.
      He'd walked miles along the coast
to find us combing the beach, then
stood, little Buddhist, with bowed head
   while we read his letter, composed
      with the help of the schoolmaster.
How could we deny the yearning
ambition to abandon the impossible
   land of his fathers, to begin again?
      We could only refuse in a silent way.
When someone asked Miles Davis
why he wouldn't play ballads anymore,
   he replied, "Because I love them too much."
      All that we never say to each other.
   The intimacies we can't complete.
Those ineluctable fragments. To be up against.

Koh Samui, Thailand

Joshua Weiner

Tokens
Thomas McGrath, 1916-1990

Out on the rough roads traveling blind
I hope to find a sign
among stars salting the night

now a black slab of meat,
bats flickering above the fields, and failing
and winging up, shades against shade,

each member of autumn's dark choir
scattering notes from the opera
of the plague year. This is not a dream.

I am a tourist through catastrophe
running towards money as if it were a train
bound for a busy station

somewhere beyond the plains.
A handful of changes. A phrase
from Madelstam: *a sound keeps on sounding*

after you disappear. A handful
of tokens now that you've disappeared
and somewhere a sign. The pernicious air

cool, unnerving, each distant isolated
light from a house or barn
marks the yawning hours,

the smell of smoke for a while
heavy from a nostalgic hearth
and gone and gone like a slight

revision on a page. With gift and meager gear
you traveled one last year
unfixed, unfinished, and wanting in the world.

Don Welch

The Unicorn

This is the shape the horse has always wanted,
free, harnessed only to myth, ridden hard
by the speculative head.

When a unicorn steps out of a horse's hooves,
it casts no shadow.

In the moonlight it is inexhaustible,
no one can run it to death.

*

For a time whatever it is moves in the wind.

The breeze has a certain flex to it,
the sky is ignited by stars.

The eyes of the unicorn are blue, circled with silver.

*

In possibility the image is always the answer.

To carry them into different countries
they were given imaginary beasts.
Some wanted to go fierce, some gentle.

Their clothes and other effects were burned,
they were put naked on unicorns.

*

Sometimes the price we pay for belief
is a thin silver coin resembling
the moon in the morning.

Its edges are soft and sharp,
it has an invisible center.

We enter by taking one step, without preparing our faces.

*

Having come a long way,
no longer riding on the original beast,
some of them had a strip of back, a piece of flank
a section of horn.

They handled them longingly.

Some of them even cried as if they knew what it was.

Jackson Wheeler

Sleeping with the Third World

As though famine, pestilence, and war were aphrodisiacs
we take our lovers from exotic places.

From Soweto to Namibia, men and women dark as pain
are irresistible in their suffering. Imagine being shot at,
losing an eye or limb, surviving torture.
They are worth their weight in cocktail conversation.

Consider the students of Lima, Santiago, Buenos Aires.
The young men with mothers or sisters named for the
mother of God. We sell their leaders guns and bombs;
and when the dissidents disappear, we plant trees,

a hedge against the future. We take lovers with skin
the color of old ivory. We feed them hamburgers
because it is American. We tell them how lucky
they are to be here, not there, where families

are killed when Union Carbide makes a mistake.
How lucky they are to be with us because we
are civilized, we save lives with collateral bombing
and know that the killing fields are far away from

Wounded Knee. How lucky they are that we saw the
advertisement announcing, "Young men and women
from exotic places anxious to meet Americans. They
appreciate someone who loves them, can show them

a good time." They will show their gratitude for
not having to worry about the next meal or whether
someone will kill them. They can be so appreciative
it's a wonder any of us sleep at night.

Paul Willis

A Miracle

I am twelve years old, sitting in the dollar seats
in the end zone, closest to the beige coliseum.
It is November, perhaps. It is 1967. It is raining

lightly, a gray sky, the usual for autumn in Oregon.
It has been raining all week long. The field
before me stretches away without lines, without

hash marks. It is a perfect churn, a caldron,
whipped into a seething of mud. The players rise
and fall before me as dark and streaming

apparitions, bubbling to the surface, sinking, all
wearing a filthy slaver. All except one. Whenever
this one takes the ball, whenever he tries to cut

the corner and sprint upfield, the men in the crowd
around me cry out, "O.J.! O.J.!" The men sound
very worried, as if someone were breaking

into their homes. They are only relieved when O.J.
slips in the mud or is just knocked down from behind.
But a miracle. He gets up–every time, when he

gets up–his uniform is shining, spotless, gold and
crimson: no dripping grime, no ooze of smudge, no
smear of earth and water, not even a trail of blood.

Mary Winters

Whoopee, It's 2000

Because we've got a mania for
    counting, for measuring.
For setting little bits and pieces off from
    other little bits and pieces.
"Millennium": because we've got a mania for naming.
For pigeonholing, for stereotyping.
We can't just let time go by
    dark light dark light dark light:
        there's got to be "seconds," "minutes," etc.

We've got to rub time's nose in itself,
    shove it up to a mirror: *look, you're 2000!*

Because we've got a mania for control:
    time's got to pass on our terms
    (it's not 2000 everywhere, you know).
Because we believe in progress, increase.
Time's got to build up, pile up,
    even topple over
    but never *start over*.

Because we like it neatly rounded off: 2000.
Because we've got a mania for great expectations:
    the two zeros in the middle are
    happy, wide open eyes.
We're facing the future squarely
    yet filled with hope; not a nuance in sight,
    nary a hesitation: 2000.

Because we like it dramatic, awesome.
Hard to imagine two thousand of anything
    –beans, buttons, bows–let alone years.
Because we like fireworks, explosions
    (hope the end-of-the-world folks aren't right).
Because we like to-ing and fro-ing but
    the pendulum's got to stop somewhere: 2000.

Because it's three ostrich eggs and one
    gimped-up hatchling.
Because it's three mounded-up treasure cars
    pulled by The Little Engine That Could.
Because the sweatshirts are swell: CLASS OF '00.
Because two is more than twice as much fun:
    ask any parent of twins.

Because we're daring the world to take us to 3000.

Carolyne Wright

The Peace Corps Volunteer Comes Home

Carrying the Kodak prints
she sent, her parents meet her
at the depot: What has she made
of the Third World?

The answer comes to her
like marked money–Brasil's
old joke: *"Café e Pelé."*
The principal exports.
She doesn't mention the color
of her lover's hands.

Her mother wrote, "Bring home
the coffee, nothing but the coffee."
She's a big girl now, she brings home
the rhythm, *Orfeo Negro*
in her walk. Her gray eyes
darkening in equatorial light.

At the Steak 'N' Ale, *feijoada*
lingers on her tongue. She waves away
the New York cut. Recife, she says,
Safety Zone. Good roads, and machetes
working through the cane.

                                        Father nods,
turns off the burglar alarms
in his thoughts. Mother brings out
the china pattern, shows
what she's added.

Neither wants to know their daughter
sleeps in the other world, dreams
in the passion flower's language,
balancing the unbroken promise
of a man's body
against her, carrying the love child,
silence, like a *figa*-charm.